27
69

ADMINISTRATIVE REFLECTIONS
FROM WORLD WAR II

ADMINISTRATIVE REFLECTIONS FROM WORLD WAR II

═━✕━═

by LUTHER GULICK

PRESIDENT, *Institute of Public Administration*
NEW YORK

UNIVERSITY, ALABAMA
UNIVERSITY OF ALABAMA PRESS

Dedicated to the Fellows of the Southern Regional
Training Program In Public Administration

GLENN ABERNATHY

PETER BERSANO

SARA BRENNAN

HELEN BRIDGMAN

GEORGE HOWARD

JAMES MOTT

ANNA QUILLEN

JOSEPH M. ROBERTSON

KENNETH VINES

BEATRICE WEAVER

FOREWORD

WITHIN THE PLANNING UNITS AND "WAR colleges" of the general staffs of the world, military men are now at work assessing their blunders and their successes in World War II, and laying out broad lines of planning for the future. All military staffs have the gruesome but inescapable responsibility of planning the most effective "defense" of their peoples in the "next war," in the event of the failure of the new machinery of permanent peace, which is even now in process of development.

Similarly politicians and students of international relations are reviewing the kaleidoscopic history of the past generation to draw from this story the new lessons of international politics, primarily as a guide for the immediate future, in a world which is afflicted with so much power politics, discord and the "insecurity jitters." These two efforts, military and political, are of course related.

Students of administration turn to this same experience, the history of World War II, but for different purposes: first, to see to what extent the generally accepted theories and "principles" of administration have found verification under the strains and stresses of war management; and second, to see what practical administrative lessons may be drawn from the tremendous array of war-time experiments, not for a future war but for application to the problems now faced internally as well as internationally. Students of administration do not need to be concerned about the "next war"—the military planners will take care of that—but they do need to be concerned with extracting from recent experience its rich harvest for the immediate management problems of a chaotic world.

This effort to draw from the recent war general administrative lessons for the present and the immediate future has this further advantage: in so doing we deal with a world now about us with many elements of certainty, while the war planners have but one fixed point, namely that any future war will be completely unlike past wars!

The lectures printed in this volume were delivered before the Fellows of the Southern Regional Training Program in Public Administration at the University of Alabama, during the latter part of November, 1946. The author treated the same theme more briefly in an address delivered at the February, 1946, meeting of the American Society for Public Administration, held in Philadelphia as the first national meeting of the Society since the end of World War II.

Though it is still too early to draw conclusions with certainty and finality from the experience of this War, it is not too early to commence the effort, knowing that others will give more searching criticism to the hypotheses thus ventured because of the effort to state the "lessons" while the experience is still fresh in the minds of many. This being the central purpose of these lectures, I have taken the liberty of stating my own present conclusions in what may be regarded by some as an unduly final and dogmatic form, hoping that this will sharpen the discussion and lead more rapidly to a winnowing out of the essential truth of our war experiences in administration. Under the circumstances I accord to others, as I reserve to myself, the right to explore further, and to restate or to negate the hypotheses I have advanced in this collection of lectures.

While I as author must accept responsibility for this volume and its contents, I wish to acknowledge my indebtedness in connection with this work to the institutions and individuals who have contributed to the studies and contacts from which these lectures grow. I owe to the University of Alabama, to the Southern Regional Training Program in Public Administration, and to Roscoe Martin the immediate occasion for the preparation of these lectures and the opportunity for their delivery under conditions both stimulating and congenial. The Institute of Public Administration and Columbia University relieved me of other assignments beginning with the Winter of 1939-1940 so that I might devote my energies to work in Washington and elsewhere in connection with the rising war emergency. This was made possible and was greatly facilitated by a grant to the Institute of Public Administration from the Carnegie Corporation for work "in the current emergency."

My opportunities for participation in and intimate observation of war emergency administration arose chiefly in connection with assignments on organizational and programming problems in the National Resources Planning Board, where I was asked to serve as the co-ordinator of post-war programs; in the Treasury, where I directed a study of Federal-State-Local fiscal relations, which covered certain aspects of war finance as well; in the War Department, where I participated in setting up the Control Division and in developing the reorganization plans of February, 1942; in the War Production Board, where I helped in developing the organizational structure of the Board and served as the head of the Office of Organizational Planning for some eight months in 1942, and as a consultant again in 1945; in the office of the Co-ordinator for Inter-American Affairs, where I was the organizer and chairman of the Advisory Committee on Education; in the Foreign Economic Administration and in the Department of State, where I was a member of the staff of the Office of Foreign Relief and Rehabilitation Operations; in the Department of Commerce, where I have been a member of the Census Advisory Committee; in the Smaller War Plants Corporation, where I was in charge of the technical aspects of the reorganization of 1944; in the United Nations Relief

and Rehabilitation Administration, where I was the
acting chief of the Secretariat at the time of its
organization; in the Bureau of the Budget where I
served in various capacities, particularly in connection with the preparation of the administrative
history of the war and the stimulation of war
histories throughout the war agencies; and finally in
the White House staff, where I was asked on a
number of occasions to aid with administrative
matters, and where I served for over a year, with
assignments on reparations which carried me through
Europe and the Pacific as far as Russia, Japan and the
Philippines, involving attendance at the Potsdam
Conference in 1945 and the meeting of the Foreign
Ministers in Paris in 1946.

I shall not endeavor to list the many individuals
who aided me and worked with me in all these and
other less formal assignments. Not only would the
list be too long, but mention of individuals might be
mistaken by some to impute to them responsibility
for what I have said in these lectures. As I have
already stated, the conclusions are purely mine and
not those of the men with whom and for whom I
have worked.

Things happen fast in time of war. Men act along
new lines boldly, decision jostling decision. Mistakes
are many, and new approaches are sudden and
frequent. This environment creates a situation
which is extraordinarily fertile in institutional
experimentation. If it is equally productive in

demonstrating what will and will not work in peace-time administration, careful attention to our war experience may prove extremely rewarding for those whose prime consideration is found in the challenging problems of peace.

LUTHER GULICK

Bronxville

CONTENTS

:: 1 ::

TIME AND TIDE

THOUGH WE ARE ALL FAMILIAR WITH THE BROAD military and political history of World War II, I plan to review that history briefly, weaving in the contemporaneously evolving pattern of American administrative developments. I do this because it is difficult to hold in the mind in proper balance these two important streams of interrelated activities: first, the stream of military, political and economic events and, second, the stream of administrative events. However it is important for our purposes in these lectures to recognize these two interrelated streams because, before we are through, it is my hope that we will be able to add further evidence to substantiate the thesis that administrative developments, like organic developments, cannot be understood unless they are related (1) to their own organic past and (2) to the compulsions of the environment in which they exist.

THE WAR BEGINS WITHOUT THE UNITED STATES

Though it was 1937 when Japan undertook its active military invasion of China, the shooting war in Europe began in September, 1939, when Germany overran Poland, and England decided to end her disastrous blunder of appeasement. In this country the European fighting gave rise to conflicting reactions. While all feared another world war, a majority of the people still thought we could keep out. Even within the government, there was no clear single policy line, though the President, Secretary Morgenthau and a few others were apparently convinced that vital American interests were sure to become involved and that war was unavoidable and imminent. They were equally determined to keep out of the war if this was possible. Thus we were preparing for war, that is for what was called "defense," and at the same time clinging to the posture of peace.

It was in this facing-both-ways atmosphere that the Mobilization Day Plan for organizing war production and the economy for war was hastily revised by the War and Navy Departments in September, 1939. Though the President promptly disbanded the board which did the work, he did set up an interdepartmental committee to co-ordinate foreign and domestic military purchases which were subjected to the "cash and carry" requirements of the revised neutrality act of November, 1939, and the British and the French were persuaded in January, 1940, to co-ordinate their war purchases in the American market.

Pressure on American industry to reduce its help to Japan and to expand our machine tool and other basic war material plants began without sanction of law in the winter of 1939-1940, even before Congress authorized export controls in mid-summer, and before new appropriations for "defense" started an upsurge of "educational contracts" through which industry was led into war production step by step, somewhat against its desires, if not against its will.

In April, 1940, Germany burst through Denmark, and rushed into Norway. In May and June, Belgium, Holland and France were crushed and the British withdrew from Dunkirk.

The President declared a state of "unlimited national emergency," urged night and day production of machine tools, set up new administations to deal with petroleum and food, and created the Office of Civilian Defense.

MAJOR ADMINISTRATIVE STEPS

In June, the President appointed two stalwart Republicans as his Secretaries of War and Navy, activated the long dormant Council of National Defense by creating the National Defense Advisory Commission, and set up a priorities committee in the Army-Navy Munitions Board. In June, 1940, Congress not only increased appropriations for defense but authorized the RFC to finance production of munitions and critical materials, and their stockpiling. Congress also approved priorities for military procurements and advance payments and negotiation in place of competitive bidding for war contracts.

During the summer, the Japanese militarists took over the government of Japan and announced their "Greater East Asia" program. While we cut off the shipment of aviation gasoline and of scrap iron to Japan, Britain, which was being subjected to the blitz "Battle of Britain," was forced, diplomatically, to close the Burma Road. Congress approved the President's plan for a "two ocean navy," enacted selective service legislation and authorized changes in the tax laws to encourage war contracts, particularly the special authorization of war production facilities. The vast Selective Service Administration came into being and the President traded 50 destroyers to Britain for island bases. Between August and October, 1940, voluntary priorities on military orders gave way to the first firm regulation as the Priorities Board was established by the Council of National Defense.

It was in the summer of 1940, also, that the President, advised by Einstein, Pegram, Sachs, Briggs and others, took action to go forward with the research and organization which produced the atomic bombs five years later, and made such remarkable advances with radar.

THE "ARSENAL OF DEMOCRACY"

In November, Roosevelt was returned to power for his third term, with wide public endorsement, due in considerable measure to the wisdom and patriotism of Wendell Willkie and his support of the

President's defense and international policies. Almost immediately, the President came forward with his "arsenal of Democracy" policy and, in January, 1941, recommended the "lend-lease" program, which received Congressional approval in March.

Parallel with these developments, the Office of Production Management was set up in place of the NDAC,[1] the status of labor in the war effort was emphasized by the partnership of Hillman in the setup on a par with Knudsen; the first mandatory priorities were established on aluminum and machine tools, the first maximum prices were set for second-hand machine tools, and the conversion of the automobile industry to aircraft production was agitated.

Narrowly failing to bring Britain to her knees, Germany turned East in April, striking into the Balkans, Greece and the Mediterranean, and finally attacking Russia in June.

EXPANDING BASIC INDUSTRIES AND FACTORY CAPACITY

During this period positive action was taken in the United States to expand aluminum and steel capacity and to begin to convert existing plants to war production, under the orders of the Supply Priorities and Allocations Board, which was superimposed over the OPM in August, 1941, to overcome the unambitious and hesitant military program, the

[1] A list of abbreviations is found in the Appendix.

military opposition to lend-lease and the then current industrial opposition to war conversion. The Office of Price Administration evolved out of the former OPACS and the Price Stabilization division of the National Defense Advisory Commission, though the OPA was not given its specific statutory powers until January, 1942, and until then depended entirely on "jawbone control."

The first Liberty Ship was launched at the end of September, 1941, and soon thereafter nonessential building construction was proscribed, the use of copper was restricted and steel plate was put under complete allocation. Labor was called to the White House to prevent further strikes and iron out other difficulties.

PEARL HARBOR AND WAR

At this point, while Japanese statesmen were in Washington to arrange a basis for peace in the Pacific, Japan struck at Pearl Harbor, crippling the antiquated American Fleet, and making it impossible for us to hold the Philippines, or aid the British in defending Singapore, the Netherlands Indies, Java, and the oil and rubber resources of the Far East.

WAR POWERS AND WAR ADMINISTRATION

This was war, total war, all over the world; and America was in it. The nation was now a unit behind the President as "Commander-in-Chief" and the Congress which had extended the draft act by a majority of one in August now declared war with but a single negative vote, the first War Powers Act was passed, and the economy drove forward to meet the President's demand for 60,000 airplanes, 45,000 tanks, 20,000 anti-aircraft guns and 8,000,000 tons of shipping. War agencies were now set up thick and fast on the loose foundations which had already been laid and under the direction of men who were already at work. The War Production Board, the War Shipping Administration, the Office of Defense Transportation, the War Manpower Commission, and the Office of War Information were established; the War and Navy Departments were extensively reorganized; the OPA was given a solid statutory basis and proceeded to control all prices and to become the administrative center for rationing tires, sugar and gasoline; and the Agricultural Adjustment Administration assumed charge of the food program as oil was brought under the Petroleum Administrator for War.

NEW PRODUCTION RECORDS AND NEW CONTROLS

Starting on the foundation laid in the educational and in the "defense" contracts, production was pushed higher and higher, and more and more bottlenecks developed in spite of the many restrictions on normal production and use of scarce materials which were established with the extension of priorities controls. By July, 1942, even the top priorities were not good enough to guarantee the delivery of materials required by shipping, munitions, lend-lease and other programs. Inflated priorities were found to be as useless as Chinese currency. The WPB was accordingly streamlined and plans were drawn for comprehensive allocations, first through the Production Requirements Plan, which was adopted in June and then by the Controlled Materials Plan adopted in November, when WPB was again reorganized on the programming and materials control side. In the meantime unemployment disappeared, labor became a major shortage, and the War Manpower Commission restricted movement of labor out of lumbering and mining, while WPB closed the gold mines in a vain effort to swing miners into copper, magnesium and other mines. The labor situation became so tense by fall that the WPB defined "critical labor areas" in which procurement officers were ordered not to place new war contracts.

It became clear that we were in danger of building more factories and shipyards than we could man, or supply with steel, copper and other scarce components, but it proved extremely difficult to dampen the construction enthusiasm of military procurement officers.

Political and economic forces threatened to carry food prices still further upward, thus threatening wage and other levels. The President quickly created the Office of Economic Stabilization in October and called in the skillful and influential Mr. James M. Byrnes to hold prices and wages together and to help persuade the country and the Congress not to upset that precarious balance.

THE TURN OF THE TIDE

From a military standpoint things continued to go badly for us through the summer of 1942. Guadalcanal in August, and Midway and the Coral Sea in October saw the end of Japanese expansion. Early in November, the Germans were turned at El Alamein to be greeted in their retreat by the North African landings. With the aid of an extraordinarily severe winter, Leningrad was saved in January, 1943, and the Germans surrendered at Stalingrad in February as the Japanese did at Guadalcanal. Tunisia fell in May, and the battle of the Atlantic with the U-boats was ended.

Thus the war turned, new fronts were opened up, the demand from the military became more and more insatiable. Synthetic rubber, high octane gasoline and the newly expanded requirements for landing craft were in violent collision; the Controlled Materials Plan went into effect and the first general scheduling order was issued; and the President set up a still higher co-ordinating office directly in the White House, the Office of War Mobilization, into which James M. Byrnes was moved. Labor transfer was restricted still further, with new controls for labor and contracts on the Pacific Coast, and subsidies were used to roll back the price of meats and butter.

MANPOWER BECOMES THE LIMITING FACTOR

The fall of 1943 brought improvements all along the line except as to manpower, which became the final irreducible bottleneck of military power and war production.   Italy surrendered in September. The USSR retook Kiev in November, and though the Germans mounted a new attack, the Russians were soon on the offensive all along the line, pressing into Poland by January as the United States was pressing the Japanese back in the Marshalls.   In America, war production reached its all-time peak in the last two months of 1943, achieving a level of almost $6 billions a month.   Though the heaviest fighting of all lay ahead, it now became clear that the initiative had passed to the Allies, that American production and Russian and American fighting had turned the scales and that Germany and Japan were being pressed back to their inescapable defeat.

RECONVERSION PLANS WITH VICTORY IN SIGHT

Though the draining off of men for the Army and Navy in the United States continued to cut production slightly and the Army demanded a comprehensive labor draft to place all labor under direct government control, the first steps were taken to lay plans for reconversion after victory.   The long secret plans of the National Resources Planning Board dealing especially with the GI's education, housing, etc., were released and the Baruch-Hancock report contributed additional plans for dealing with contract termination and reconversion. Donald Nelson issued his policy statement on reconversion in March, 1944, and finally released his "four orders" permitting certain reconversion activities, in June, in the face of terrible opposition by the military who feared that such discussions might lessen the keen edge of our final thrust to victory. Rome was occupied and the historic invasion of France was carried through with spectacular success. Congress enacted the GI Bill of Rights as nationwide manpower priorities were set up by the War Manpower Commission, making use of the Area Production Urgency Committees of the WPB which had gradually been extended to the tight areas from the first beginnings on the Pacific Coast. Special manpower shortages developed in the foundries and in the heavy tire lines, for which the Army was persuaded to release skilled workers.

The controversy of policies and personalities as between the Army and the War Production Board, and within American industry as between those who were in a position to reconvert and those who were not, flared into the open and was solved by accepting the resignations of the two men who had brought the industrial machine to its unbelievable production peak, Nelson and Wilson, and the establishment of Mr. Byrnes by statute at the head of the Office of War Mobilization and Reconversion.

MILITARY REVERSES AND HYSTERIA

The whole war production picture was then given a new urgency by the turn of military affairs. In October, 1944, the Philippines were invaded, and vast supplies and shipping were in demand from the Pacific as the bombing drive on Japan began in earnest.

In November, General Eisenhower opened the drive on the Siegfried Line, only to be met, as he was preparing to storm the Rhine, by a fierce German counter thrust, which grew into the ominous "Bulge." At this point the Army became hysterical over the rumored lack of supplies and equipment in France, and all prior talk of reconversion was submerged. The OWMR, into which General Lucius Clay had been absorbed as deputy, restricted horse racing, instituted brown-outs, tightened rationing, used priorities to enforce manpower ceilings, and finally mandated a curfew for civilians. Four aluminum plants were reopened, and many war contracts were extended which had been slated for termination. It was even proposed to build new plants to manufacture heavy ammunition, though these were finally stopped as the Bulge collapsed in January.

RENEWED MILITARY TRIUMPHS

In February, Russia crossed the Oder River, and in March the Americans crossed the Rhine. The German economy went into complete collapse as internal transportation all but failed. The WPB talked again about reconversion, and a working committee was appointed on Period I, to reorganize production controls when Germany surrendered. In April, Okinawa was invaded, the Russians entered Berlin and the United States and USSR forces met at Torgau, the Americans thrusting across Germany with extraordinary mobility and tactical skill.

DEATH OF ROOSEVELT

Though Franklin Roosevelt died on April 12, the plans for victory, to which he had contributed more than any other one man, were complete. While more men in more parts of the world than ever before in history felt the sudden pangs of personal loss on the death of one man, even this sorrow did not delay the swift pace or rhythm of Allied advance.

THE GERMAN SURRENDER

Mussolini was caught and executed in Italy as the Germans surrendered there, and early in May with the disappearance of Hitler and his closest associates in the debris of Berlin, Admiral Doenitz surrendered all German forces unconditionally.

The V-E Day plans were immediately released in the United States. Gasoline rationing was relaxed, as were the curfew and racing bans. The Army announced its redeployment plans looking toward the immediate transfer of the seasoned fighting units from Europe to the Orient, with re-equipment for their new assignments, with more flame throwers and light armor for the new combat tactics.

Many industry orders which had stood since 1942 were revoked, the Controlled Materials Plan was "open ended," and certain of the restrictions on construction were removed to hasten factory reconversion and the construction of housing. Though the Price Administrator urged a less precipitate abandonment of controls as a bulwark against inflation he found no effective support in the OWMR, the WPB, the White House or the Congress.

In June, as the San Francisco Conference creating the UN Charter came to a successful end, the War Department made a 50 per cent cut-back in artillery contracts, and the WPB announced the end of priorities and CMP in October. The War Manpower Commission reduced the number of "critical labor areas," preparatory to its abandonment of all controls in August.

THE JAPANESE SURRENDER

Following the reparations discussions in Moscow in July and the general discussions in Potsdam in July and August, 1945, Japan received her final ultimatum, the atomic bombs, and the blow of Russia's war declaration, and surrendered on August 14. This was the official end of the fighting. Thousands of war contracts were terminated by telegram; the WMC rescinded all controls and was promptly abolished through absorption into the

Department of Labor. The WPB canceled 210 of 340 industry orders; ODT removed all controls, lend-lease was suspended; gasoline rationing was revoked; the petroleum controls were removed; and the Foreign Economic Administration was abolished and its remaining activities turned over to the State Department, the Commerce Department, the Department of Agriculture, and the RFC.

In September, as Germany, Japan and Austria were "occupied," WPB and OWMR ended all lumber controls and set construction free. At the close of the month the Controlled Materials Plan was ended, and nothing remained but a few simple priorities to support the continuing military contracts.

On November 4, WPB itself was abolished, as its remaining activities became the Civilian Production Administration.

This is as good a date as any to select as signalizing the end of this war administration chronology.

OUTSTANDING FEATURES OF THE STORY

I do not know what the effect upon your mind and your emotions is of this turbulent story of events, but for me, four things stand out: the omnipresent imminence of chaos and the narrowness of our escape from disaster and defeat; the intricate and half understood interdependence of social, economic, political, military and even climatic and personality factors; the continuity of relationships, and the conditioning of organizations and policies and men by their own yesterdays; and finally the extraordinary effectiveness achieved in total war by the peace-loving and discipline-hating American people.

When I let my mind pore over these complex events, I have the feeling of multiplicity and confusion; that no historian will ever make a clear synthesis of these days, without omitting more than he neatly extracts. And yet, there is a grand pattern; and each event, big or small, can be shown to be organically tied to its own past and future, and at the same time, causally related to its current surroundings. But neither these causal relations to the environment, nor the organic relations to the past, appear to have determined the succeeding steps. At every point alternatives crowded the stage, and *decisions* not written in the script were made by the actors. When we study administration, therefore, what we have before us is the record of decisions, opportunistic or planned, bringing some order out of chaos along the path of human purpose. What we must look for are the co-ordinating principles and techniques by which purposes have been achieved. We must examine the teamwork pattern and the evolving machinery of administrative management, and discover, if we can, the causes of administrative success and failure. This project will occupy us in the following lectures.

∗II∗

WAR RESOURCES
AND
THEIR CO-ORDINATED UTILIZATION

YESTERDAY WE TRACED A PICTURE OF GERMANY
and Japan taking to arms aggressively in order
to crush their competitors and assure to themselves domination of a major part of the world
around them, if not ultimately of the whole world.

Germany almost succeeded, and was stopped only
by her own bad planning and a combination of the
fighting spirit and political ability of England, the
courage and vastness and cold of Russia, and the
fighting and producing abilities of the United States
and Canada. In the meantime, Japan, which had
gambled mistakenly on a short war and a negotiated
peace, was destroyed by the United States almost
singlehanded.

Thus mankind turned a corner in world history, a
corner as important as the fall of Rome, Columbus'
trip to the New World, or the Industrial Revolution.

Yesterday we sketched in broad outlines the history
of these war years, noting especially the administrative agencies which were created in the United States
to enable the American people to make their decisive

contribution to the defeat of Germany and Japan, and to harness the horses which have brought mankind " 'round the mountain."

It would be only natural if I have left you in some confusion; this period of history has been characterized by confusion. Until 1943, our war activities were largely dictated by the aggressive successes of our enemies. And the leading spirit of the victorious United Nations, Franklin Delano Roosevelt, with all his extraordinary sense of timing in political strategy, was still a pragmatist, relying on improvisation and adaptation. Under the circumstances this history was confused. If I should make it seem all clear, simple, and logical, you would know that my analysis was superficial and misleading.

However, it is possible to approach the question of war resources and their mobilization, not solely from the background of military history and the kaleidoscope of administrative experiments, but also from the nature and interrelations of the resources themselves. I think you will find that this approach furnishes students of administration with a somewhat more meaningful frame of reference for the appraisal of America's experience than the historical drama I attempted to present in yesterday's discussion.

WAR RESOURCES

What then does a nation fight with in modern war? What does it use? What resources does it rely on for victory?

Though the answer to these questions may be arranged in various ways, it would certainly contain the following seven major elements:

I. The Armed Services

Including, of course, the Army, the Navy, the Air Forces, the Coast Guard, the Militia, and any other Military or Quasi-Military organizations.

II. Other Nations

Who may be drawn in as Allies to fight too, or as friendly "neutrals" to aid with food, shipping, raw materials, or even more aggressively. Foreign investments, in accessible lands, are a distinct asset.

III. Manpower

The indispensable basis of action and power, a resource measured in sheer numbers, and in health and vitality; subject to increased effectiveness through training and discipline; and capable of extraordinary enhancement through teamwork and spiritual devotion to common purposes.

IV. Raw Materials

Those taken out of the ground through mining and otherwise; the minerals and chemicals, the fuels—coal, petroleum, and fissionable elements; and the food and other products which come from the forests, agriculture and animal husbandry. In this area, both stock-piles and the rate of internal production are important, as are opportunity of import.

V. Capital Investments

Including factories and tools, power installations, the transportation system, cities and their utilities, housing, the whole communications system, with telephone, telegraph, radio, newspaper presses, all the machinery of business, and all the inventory in process of manufacture or on the shelves of merchants, or stored up in the factories and homes.

VI. Science, Technology and Research

Not only the know-how of production, but also the know-

how-to-solve new problems of military and industrial technology; invention and organized research into pure and applied
science; and research into social, political, administrative and
economic facts, both abroad and at home.

VII.   Organization and Institutions
   Including government, and the structure, know-how and
discipline of government; economic institutions, with property,
production and distribution, money, wages, prices, contracts,
credit, interest, taxes, etc.; social institutions, with the community, the family, the shop, and organizations of industry,
labor, education, science, religion, politics, and organizations for
citizen service or group action.

These, I believe, are the seven great categories of
national strength upon which a people can draw to
save itself in time of war.   They are in summary: the
Armed Services, international friends, manpower,
raw materials, investments, science and technology,
and organization and institutions.   These are the
national resources for war—and also for peace.

ORGANIZATION IN RELATION TO RESOURCES AND
TIME

Though I have been warned of the dangers of
"chartism" and the tendency to oversimplify events
and relationships through ideological tables, which
may be said to "place the chart before the horse,"
I am going to ask you to look at the accompany-
ing diagram of war resources and developing war
machinery.   As you see, the left-hand column of this
chart presents the seven major war resources of the
nation.   The successive columns, from left to right,
stand for time, running from 1940 to 1945.   At the

TIME TABLE OF ADMINISTRATIVE ORGANIZATION FOR WAR

WAR AGENCIES CLASSIFIED BY MAJOR NATIONAL RESOURCE EFFECTED AND BY DATE OF ESTABLISHMENT

(A list of abbreviations is found in the appendix. The year of dissolution appears in parenthesis.)

NATIONAL RESOURCES FOR WAR	1940 J F M A M J J A S O N D	1941 J F M A M J J A S O N D	1942 J F M A M J J A S O N D	1943 J F M A M J J A S O N D	1944 J F M A M J J A S O N D	DATE OF ABANDONMENT. OR REORGANIZATION
ARMED SERVICES						
Major Coordinating Agencies			JCS			(JCS '47)
Army	WD		RF'ORG			Defense Department (Created 1947)
Air Forces	WD ND		REORG	BuA		
Navy	ND · BuS		P & M · C & O			
Coast Guard	CG	to ND	MInsp			To Treas '46
Intelligence Service	WD ND StD		OSS			(OSS '46)
Other	USTC		ASF			
INTERNATIONAL	StD					(WRB '45) (UNRRA '47)
Political and Economic	XOP	AExC CIAA	DAR OLLA · CSAB WPB USCC CPRB OFRRO	UNRRA	WRB	(USCC '45) (CPRB '46)
Military		EDB BEO BEW	CRMB CFB · IADB MAB · CCS	FEA OWMR	OIAA	(CIAA '45) (FEA '45) (MAB '45)
MANPOWER						(WMC '45)
Programming	Lab NDAC	OPM	WMC	OWM OWMR · APUC		
Conscription	SSS		WMC	WMC · SSS		
Allocation			WMC			
Employment Service	USES	FEPC	WMC			
Wage Control			NWLB			
Discipline		NDMB	NWLB WMC			(NWLB '46)
Training	TWI				RRA	
Health	USPHS · HMC CHW			CPF		
Information and Morale	OGR OEM	Inf FEPC ODHW · OCD CI OFF OC	OWI			(OC '45) (OWI '45) (FEPC '46)
MATERIALS AND PRODUCTS	Int					(WPB '45)
Programming	ANMB NDAC	OPM	WPB	OWM OWMR		
Production Control			WPB	APUC		
Distribution Control		PBCND	WPB			
Coal			WPB SFCW	SFAW CMA		
Petroleum		OPCW	WPB · PAW	PRC		(PAW '46)
Food	Ag AAA NDAC		WPB	WFA		(WFA '45)
Rubber	RRC		WPB · ORD	RDC		
Ships	USMC					(DSC '45)
Stockpiles	ANMB RFC · MRC DSC		WPB			(MRC '45)
FACTORIES AND FACILITIES	Com					(WPB '45)
Programming	ANMB NDAC	OPM · SPAB	WPB	OWM OWMR		
Construction			WPB			
Conversion			WPB			
Allocation			WPB			
Tools						
Power Installations	Int		WPB			
Transportation, land	ICC NDAC	ODT	WPB			(ODT '47)
Transportation, ocean	USMC		WPB WSA			(WSA '46)
Communications	FCC	DCB	WPB · BWC			
Utilities			WPB			
Housing	USHA DHC	DDHC	WPB NHA			
SCIENCE AND TECHNOLOGY						
Pure Science and Research	NRC NDRC	OSRD				(OSRD '47)
Applied Science and Invention			OPRD			
Management and Administration	BB OEM		WPU	OPS		
ORGANIZATION AND INSTITUTIONS	XOP					(OWMR '47)
Coordinating	BB NDAC	OPM · SPAB	WPB OES	CCPA OWM OWMR		(OES '47)
Prices	NRPB OEM NDAC	OPACS	OPA OES	OWM OWMR		
Wages		OPM	NWLB OES	OWM OWMR		
Credit and Financing	RFC DPC		USCC			
Taxation	Treas					
Contracts	NDAC		WPB		WCPAB OCS	(SWPC '45)
Industrial Structure	JD		SWPC			(OCD '45) (PWRC '46)
Citizen Service	ARC NDAC	USO OCD CAP	PWRC	OCWS		(APC '45)
Other	NDAC	CAS	APC WRA		SWPA	(CAS '45) (WRA '46)

beginning of 1940 I indicate in a general way the major agencies then in existence. However the main purpose of the chart is to show the timing of the creation of the emergency war agencies. These are shown opposite the major resource affected. Thus we can see what resources were brought under various intensities of mobilization and when.

While it is not possible on any chart covering so vast a development to show anything except a few major facts, these may serve to help us weave in the more subtle texture in our consideration of the web of events.

With the aid of this chart, it is possible to trace generally the important developments. For example, the public information function, listed here under manpower, and "morale," was initially dealt with through the Executive Office of the President, the Office of Government Reports, the Office for Emergency Management and various departmental information officers. In May, 1941, the Office of Civilian Defense took over a part of the responsibility, shortly before the Co-ordinator of Information was set up. In October, the Office of Facts and Figures was created with stronger powers of co-ordination. This was superseded in June, 1942, by the Office of War Information, which had the general responsibility for public information at home and abroad and the duty to clear and co-ordinate reports, though it did not supersede or direct the reports issued by the military, the State Department, and the White House. Another agency operating partly in the morale area was the Office of Censorship, which was established immediately after Pearl Harbor.

Glancing down the 1942 column it is interesting to note almost contemporaneous creation of the War Production Board, the War Manpower Commission, and the War Labor Board, the statutory establishment of the Office of Price Administration, the reorganization of the War Department, the Air Forces and the Navy, the establishment of the War Shipping Administration, and the creation of the Joint and Combined Chiefs of Staff and various international "combined Boards." Later that year, we see the creation of three czardoms in rubber, agriculture and petroleum, with a partial transfer of program responsibilities from the WPB. This split led to the establishment, six months later, of a White House co-ordinating agency, the Office of War Mobilization.

Thus the erection of war agencies and the expansion of regular departments to meet war needs went forward in waves beginning in the late spring of 1940, with important advances early in 1941 and again in the fall. Then came Pearl Harbor, with an important series of far-reaching changes following almost immediately. During the latter half of 1942, specialized agencies were set up to deal with specialized difficulties, especially synthetic rubber, food and petroleum, and a little later, coal. This split-up of activities, as well as the split between wages and prices and the competition between military and civil agencies, called for a series of top co-ordinating agencies at the White House level as has been noted, with the Office of War Mobilization appearing in June, 1943. With this development the war organization was complete, though various shifts and changes of title were subsequently made.

The situation as it then existed has been well summarized by James W. Fesler as follows:

By mid-1943, when the war organization of the Federal Government was stabilized, there were five kinds of agencies: (1) Old-line, civilian departments and commissions, largely shunted aside, robbed of their most imaginative personnel, and at best used in research and advisory capacities without decision-making authority in war matters. Examples are the Department of Labor, Interior, Commerce, and Agriculture, and the Federal Power Commission; (2) war-swollen permanent departments and commissions, like the War and Navy Departments and Maritime Commission; (3) emergency agencies focusing attention entirely on a single commodity or industry, like the Petroleum Administration for War, Solid Fuels Administration for War, and Office of the Rubber Director; (4) emergency agencies with "horizontal directive authority" over a major defense function—like the War Production Board, War Manpower Commission, Office of Price Administration, and Foreign Economic Administration; (5) super-co-ordinating agencies like the Office of War Mobilization, Office of Economic Stabilization, Office for Emergency Management, Bureau of the Budget, and White House.[2]

[2] James W. Fesler, November 8, 1946. Southern Political Science Association, Knoxville.

PRELIMINARY OBSERVATIONS

In concluding this discussion of national resources and their progressive administrative mobilization for war in the United States from 1940 through to the summer of 1943, I wish to make a number of preliminary observations before endeavoring, in the following lectures, to draw some lessons from the war.

As to Resources.—As to the resources we have discussed, it is important for our purposes to note four central facts:

(1) The *resources are strictly limited* in any war situation under each category. The number of adult men and women is strictly limited; the supply of coal or petroleum or timber is restricted; the factories and tools are generally short; there is seldom a super-abundance of food; and scientific knowledge and know-how are scarce. Each of these resources has its limits, limits which must be taken into account in waging war, and planning offensive or defensive actions.

(2) However, these *resources are extensively "intermutable,"* that is they can be changed from one into another when this is essential. For example, a shortage of petroleum can be made up with the distillation of coal; a shortage of rubber can be made up with polymerization of petroleum; a shortage of cotton can be made good with wood fibre; a shortage of nitrates from mines can be solved through elec-

trical fixation of the air; a shortage of ships can be made up by the use of steel, shipyards and manpower; a lack of food can be overcome with fertilizer, manpower, and farm tools, or with the use of ships, or even with chemical treatment of wood. While the ultimate resource is manpower, even this can in effect be expanded by machinery, better technology, an enlarged labor force, education and heightened morale. Germany went so far as to import slave labor, thus converting territorial victories into workers.

(3) While limited resources are thus extensively intermutable, *four things are necessary for the interchange* in time of war. These are (a) comparative *surpluses* in certain categories; (b) technological and administrative *know-how;* (c) *manpower;* and (d) *time.* In other words, the conversion from oil or coal to rubber cannot be made unless a nation has coal or oil and manpower which can be spared, administrative skill, practical knowledge on how to proceed and time to do the job. The problem becomes doubly difficult because in almost every case new factories are required and workers must be trained, thus involving still more direct and indirect shortage items.

(4) In a prolonged "total war," *the manufacture of substitutes* not only uses men and time, but *creates new shortages* in new directions. The only resource I can think of which was in adequate supply every-

where was air! Thus the calculus of war has become
the computation of the probable marginal utility of
intermutable national resources within the compulsions of an imperious time-table. The final elements
in this calculus are manpower and time.

Crucial Place of Administration.—This being so,
it becomes clear that the strength of a nation in time
of war is directly conditioned by its management
competence. To make the most of its available
resources, a nation must plan, decide and execute the
best possible programs for placing the right number
of men in the armed forces, in the war factories, in
the factories which keep the economy going, in
agriculture, in transportation, and in research and
professional education. Similarly steel must be
allocated to shells, tanks, new factories, airplane
engines, nails, frying pans and bobby pins. Petroleum
must be divided wisely between military use and
civilian use, between 100 octane gasoline, furnace oil,
and the rubber program. Furthermore each of these
decisions and allocations must fit the other. That is,
the steel allocations must fit the copper allocations,
the fuel allocations, the power allocations, the manpower allocations, and on a set time scale.

In a world war, all of these questions are complicated by the needs and demands of allies, and by
the shifting fortunes of war, especially when important overseas resources are lost, or new weapons
and techniques emerge in the laboratories of the
researchers or in the hands of the enemy.

This difficult task of planning and replanning, of deciding and revising programs, and of organizing and directing the work to produce the best co-ordinated end result—this is administration. If it is poorly done, with poor co-ordination and bad teamwork, with internal conflicts, with blunders in the assignment of scarce resources, the creation of destructive bottlenecks, and stubborn refusal to make adjustments, with errors in the assessment of time factors, and with mistaken notions of risk and strength, a nation will fall short of realizing its maximum potential, and may in the process lose a war, and its place in history. Thus at the center of the problem of war resources is the problem of administration.

As to the Rhythm of Organization.—In spite of the apparent, and at times real, confusion in the expansion of old agencies, the creation of new agencies, and the general flow of seemingly overlapping and conflicting alphabetical units during the war years, it is possible to trace two fairly clear lines of action. The *first* is the gradual drive toward a comprehensive war machine with independent major operating units for each of the major types of national war resources, and with co-ordinating mechanisms within the total structure designed to bring about balanced integration of planning, decision and execution. The *second* is the sequence of this evolution, the rhythm of growth and adaptation, starting with (a) planning and advisory agencies,

(b) passing to action agencies with extensive power of issuing co-ordinating directives to other action agencies, (c) improvising bottleneck-breaking agencies for individual programs and then (d) correcting the conflicts thus engendered by setting up co-ordinating agencies of limited jurisdiction, and finally (e) creating a super-co-ordinating agency in the White House, with complete authority over the domestic economy.

The Time Factor.—It was a common saying in Washington during the war that "You may count on getting reorganized every six months, but the show goes on." A glance at the chart above shows these periods of major reorganization activity:

1940, June and July
1941, January, July, August, and December
1942, January, February, July, October, and November
1943, March, April, May, and November
1944, February and July

Though the rhythm of reorganization thus does seem to fall in waves which are very roughly four to seven months apart, a major upset in the pattern occurred, of course, immediately after Pearl Harbor. The year 1942 as a whole showed more organization and reorganization than any other period. However, internal reorganization tended to show a more regular rhythm than did the structure of the government as a whole. For example, the dates of change in the WPB in 1942 were in January, July, and November. The corresponding important dates in OPA were January, March, May, and December.

As far as I know, no one has made a careful study of this time factor in organizational evolution. Those who were "on the inside" in Washington during the war will doubt that there is any definite time factor involved, as there is, for example, in growing a tree. They would point to external events, like Pearl Harbor, the adjournment of Congress, the date of an election, or a strike or snowstorm as influencing a major administrative decision. They would call attention to the part played by individual personalities, some of whom accepted emergency war appointments after long delay, and then proceeded to bring about important administrative reorganizations in two to three months as they took hold of their assignments.

Another factor influencing the timing in setting up specific organizations was the President's span of attention. In every case, except the war agencies created by Congress, namely the OPA, the Smaller War Plants Corporation and the Selective Service Administration, the final time decision was entirely the President's, though some of his moves, such as the creation of the Rubber Director, were greatly influenced by the activities of Congressional committees. The President was a busy man. Frequently an administrative order, which he had called for in broad terms, would lie on his desk for weeks and months before final revision and issuance. At times these delays were intentional; but at other times it seemed as though they were due solely to there being not enough hours in the day.

The newspapers have frequently observed that every new agency goes through its "honeymoon period" during which the new establishment is given the benefit of the doubt, and is not expected to deliver. I am convinced that this also enters into the timing of war organization. No matter how bad an organization is, or poor the appointee who heads it— and the two may not go together—two to three months are allowed for the honeymoon, two months are needed to crack up, or for events to outgrow the agency, and another month is needed to take action along a new line. This adds up to the traditional six months!

But lying back of these conditioning factors were two fundamental causal forces. These were, of course, (1) enemy action and (2) the progressive tightening of the entire economy. For example, as soon as the war started, censorship was required, the control of transportation was called for, and power was given to the President to control production, prices, factories and the flow of materials. Therefore, organizations were set up to do these things. Then, as the collisions between programs became more and more numerous, as ships competed with tanks for steel, and airplanes and rubber competed for petroleum, new controls were required to bring into the most effective balance the use of scarce materials and manpower. When this happened, new administrative structures were set up. Thus the underlying reasons for action were found in the pressure of circumstances, the inevitable changes of the war economy, though the precise time of action may have been influenced by personal, political and administrative factors.

Another controlling factor is, of course, public opinion. Neither the President nor the Price Administrator nor the Selective Service Administrator nor the Commissioner of Internal Revenue can enforce a policy effectively without substantial public support. Thus the time required to educate the public up to a new program becomes an essential step in the inauguration of the new policy. This of itself imposes an inescapable time imperative because education like yeast takes time. It was precisely at this point that the nature of the Japanese attack on the American Navy made it possible for the American Government to develop its war potential with such effectiveness and speed.

As to the Expendability of Organizations and Men.—Organizations and the men who are selected to direct them are expendable. In a world of unprecedented emergencies and uncharted experiments, many things must be tried. When some fail to meet the situation, or when they have served their immediate purpose, the organizations and the men used must be superseded. They are casualties, sacrificed in the process of institutional maneuvering. Many a time, also, an organization or a man is forced to walk the plank up forward to feed the sharks while the ship's engineer goes overboard to fix the rudder, safe from attack.   Perhaps more common is the "trial balloon," designed to test out a doubtful idea, the receptivity of public opinion, Congressional reaction, or the accuracy of the timing of a new program. Sometimes, also, organizations are used up to educate the public; they are designed to dramatize the need for a new line of action.   By the time they have served their purpose, they may be considerably worse for wear.   Still another expendable is the organization, or the man, who is used to fight a necessary jurisdictional battle, but who in the process, even after victory, cannot be continued because he has built up such terrific antagonisms that he cannot function effectively in the new situation.   Thus it comes about especially in a popular government like ours that organizations and men in time of war are no less expendable than are their colleagues fighting on land, sea or air.

Behind all this, students of administration must recognize an imperative political necessity.   We used to say, "the king can do no wrong."   Now we recognize that the prestige of top management must be maintained even though this involves a certain shifting of responsibility for individual failures and successes to subordinate organizations and men.   This is cruel to those organizations and men, but it preserves the integrity of total management in a world of trial-and-error.   In administration, as in baseball, it is the batting average that counts, not the occasional strikeout. The top management must be held accountable on the total record, not on each segment.

Comparison with Original War Mobilization Plans.—It is interesting to compare the final war administration thus developed by mid-1943 with the original War Mobilization Plan.[3] The general outline of the original plan is set forth in the left-hand column of the following tabulation, while the right-hand column shows what was actually done.

1939 War Mobilization Plan	1940 to 1943 Developments
Public Relations Administration, to co-ordinate the dissemination of information and maintain high morale.	Office of War Information, also engaged in overseas dissemination.
Selective Service Administration, to induct men into the armed services.	Selective Service System
War Labor Administration, to provide for the equitable and voluntary distribution of labor between industry and agriculture, and between war and non-war industries.	War Manpower Commission, War Labor Board, Office of Economic Stabilization, Committee on Fair Employment Practices, Area Production and Manpower Urgency Committees, Office of War Mobilization.

[3] Industrial Mobilization Plan, Senate Doc. 134, October, 1939, somewhat revised in November.

War Trade Administration, to regulate imports and exports for war purposes.

Board for Economic Warfare, which became the Office for Economic Warfare, and the Foreign Economic Administration; United States Commodity Corporation; Office of Foreign Relief and Rehabilitation Operations, which became UNRRA; Office of Lend-Lease Administration; Combined Raw Materials Board, and other Combined Boards.

War Finance Administration to advise the President on all financial policies and co-ordinate tax, credit and inflation, debt policies and flow of capital, public and private.

No specific fiscal co-ordinating agency established; Office of War Mobilization and Reconversion acquired general authority in this area.

Price Control Authority, to determine price policies, leaving their administration to the permanent and temporary agencies concerned, relying chiefly on "voluntary co-operative pressure" except in cases of profiteering.

Office of Price Administration, with complete control over prices, cost subsidies to keep prices down, operating under the Office of Economic Stabilization and the Office of War Mobilization.

Rationing of tires, sugar, shoes, gasoline, furnace oil, coffee, fats, etc., through OPA machinery under orders from WPB and OWMR.

Wage controls under the War Labor Board, the Office for Economic Stabilization and the OWMR.

War Resources Administration, to plan and enforce wartime industrial mobilization, to co-ordinate military with non-military requirements; to issue priorities and allocate plants to procurement agencies. The following divisions are mentioned: facilities, commodities, power and fuel, transportation. Advisory War Services Committees are created for each major industrial group. Procurement is left with the services.

War Production Board, with the top power over priorities and allocations of critical materials and facilities; with some division of authority over rubber, food, oil. Office of Defense Transportation; War Food Administration. Top co-ordination of policies shifted to the Office of War Mobilization.

Advisory War Industry Committees. Procurement left with the services, the Maritime Commission, the Treasury and the War Food Administration.

Allocation of materials and components, not of facilities.

Reconversion from war to peace was noted as "a very important secondary wartime consideration." No specific machinery for reconversion was recommended, though it was hinted that the WRA might function in this capacity.

Reconversion plans by NRPB, the Congress, WPB, OPA, Department of Labor, WMC, Department of Agriculture, and finally by the OWMR. Most controls abandoned soon after V-J Day.

It is evident from this very brief comparison that the industrial mobilization planners had a rather hazy picture of modern total war and of the industrial and economic controls which it would require. As a result they also underestimated the importance of political leadership and thought that the President could be persuaded to delegate the operation to a single all-powerful administrator drawn from the "patriotic business leaders of the Nation." They provided no food administration initially and thought that price control "may be required." No economic dealings with allies were apparently contemplated, and though mobilization was recognized as an evolutionary process, the war planners did not envision, even in mid-1939, our crab-like progress into "defense" and war.

One strong recommendation of the mobilization planners was not carried out. This was the suggestion for the creation of a War Finance Administration. Nothing of the sort was developed, though the OWMR was given certain ineffective power over the co-ordination of financial, tax and other programs. The Bureau of the Budget exercised some influence over the spendings, price, deficit, tax, and debt discussions. The Credit policy was influenced by the RFC, the Smaller War Plants Corporation, the USCC and other corporations, the procurement agencies, the WPB, and the Board for Economic Warfare; and consumer credit was limited by the Federal Reserve Board. The Treasury managed the debt and pressed for action by Congress on tax matters, but without great success, as Congress rejected the fiscal arguments of the Treasury, the Budget Bureau, and the OPA.

Except for this single departure from the War Mobilization recommendations, the final administrative system may be said to cover all of the functions recommended by the 1939 planners, though the final structure was far more extensive as the controls were far more complete. This is a further evidence of the comprehensive character of the American war administration as developed by the middle of 1943.

IN SUMMARY

When a nation goes to war, it girds itself for the supreme test. In so doing it can call on its military forces, its international friends, its own manpower, its raw materials, its factories, tools and inventories, its scientific and technical abilities, and its political, economic and social institutions and skills.

These resources are strictly limited, extensively intermutable, provided you have time, and, in a continued and exhausting war, end up with bottlenecks and shortages all across the board. The final elements in the equation are time and manpower.

The development of maximum power thus depends upon the co-ordinated management of these resources, and therefore upon organization and administration.

The United States as late as mid-1941 hoped for peace, and was determined not to be drawn into a world war if it could be avoided without jeopardizing essential American interests. Therefore we did not organize for war until after we were attacked. Thus our administrative structure for war, which we have examined both historically and from the standpoint of the resources concerned, was not established like a new building and completed before occupancy, but was built while occupied and re-modeled from time to time as we waged the war. This evolutionary approach to war organization is apparently inevitable for a peaceful democracy.

Nevertheless, the final result of our development was a war administrative structure which contained action agencies and co-ordinating agencies covering and controlling in various degrees all of the major national resources. The only important activity planned for which was not provided in the end was an agency for the co-ordination and direction of fiscal policy. There were, however, many crucial activities and agencies, the need for which had not been foreseen.

The sequence and rhythm of institutional develop-ment shows a progression with six to eight months time interval, running from planning agencies, through action agencies, to co-ordinating agencies. This periodicity and sequence, though anticipated in most cases by prior plans and by some prognostica-tors, can be fully explained only by the pressure of circumstances under the impact of enemy action on the one hand and the progressive tightening of the economy on the other. In the process many men and many organizations were of necessity found expendable. It is not necessary to assume that there was a "grand comprehensive design."

None the less, whether partly because of design, or primarily because of the pressure of events, the United States did achieve a reasonably comprehensive administrative structure for war by mid-1943. We will turn in the following lectures to examine the achievements and the failures of this administrative structure, and to indicate, where we can, the lessons which may be learned from this experience by students of administration.

‥III‥

ACHIEVEMENTS AND FAILURES
IN THE MANAGEMENT OF WAR

IN ONE SENSE, IT IS ALWAYS TOO EARLY TO WRITE
or talk about an important recent historical
event. Those who do so must proceed without
the knowledge of many important facts which are
still "secret," and without the benefit of a great deal
of fundamental analysis in special fields, analysis
which must be woven together to permit men to
perceive the true pattern of events in proportion and
balance. There is, moreover, nothing like the
passage of time to show what was and what was not
important in a series of interdependent activities.
However, something is to be said for the early though
somewhat brash attempt to draw broad conclusions
from events. Such conclusions may have some
validity to help our thinking immediately, and to the
extent that they are inadequate, they will stimulate
others to expand or refute the ideas presented. In
the inquiry on which we are here engaged, it is hardly
possible to draw administrative lessons from the war
experience, as we will do in the final lecture, unless
we have reached some rather clear judgments as to
what were and what were not successful manage-

ment operations. Our own private conclusions as to the achievements and failures of the war effort thus become the basis for judging war organization and administration. It is better to state these success-and-failure judgments specifically at this point than to leave them unexpressed and thus masked in the background of our argument. In doing so one must reserve the right to revise these hypotheses as further facts and analysis become available in the course of history.

MAJOR FAILURES

It is never comforting to take a penetrating look at one's failures. But it can be instructive. That is the purpose of the following comments. Accordingly American management failures in World War II are outlined under four headings: the failure to learn from World War I, failures in military affairs, failures in domestic affairs, and failures in foreign affairs.

Failure to Learn from World War I.—As we look back now we can see how little we learned up to 1940 from World War I. As a nation we were in 1939 still like the proverbial ostrich with our head in the sand. However we were no worse than Great Britain, whose international policy blunders from 1930 to 1939 meted out for England so tragic a fate. We did learn the folly of mass hysteria in war. We also came to the realization that peace requires world collaboration no less than war, and that successful joint effort is made up of joint work at the technical level and requires the adjustment of international political problems through public discussion in the light of world opinion, not solely through secret diplomacy and the eternal maintenance of the *status quo*. Perhaps even more important than this was the hard lesson that international policy must be genuinely non-partisan, and that the President and the Senate and the leaders of both political parties must work together with the same national objectives. It is not safe to play personal politics with international stakes.

On this point I remember very well a conversation with President Franklin D. Roosevelt in the summer of 1937. The last volume of Ray Stannard Baker's *Woodrow Wilson—Life and Letters* lay open on his desk. He turned the conversation from my business to Woodrow Wilson, and said: "You know, Wilson made just one mistake: he failed to do the things that were required to bring the Senate along." Many times after that, when people were baffled by Roosevelt's political sacrifices and maneuvers, it seemed to me that his actions could be understood, and even predicted, from the policy clue given by these words. Franklin Roosevelt was determined that there should be no failure of the Senate and the President to work together on foreign affairs later on, and no danger that the Senate would fail to ratify his peace treaties and the international agencies he was hoping to build in the footsteps of Woodrow

Wilson. Nor was Roosevelt the only man who had learned this political lesson from World War I.

We learned a few things also on the military side. We knew that we could not recruit an Army fairly without a draft, and adopted the selective service act 18 months before we were actually at war. However we were very slow to take to heart the air-power lessons of the war, even after watching what the Germans did in Spain. We were similarly slow in realizing what mechanization would do to war, and were still psychologically in the trenches and behind the Maginot Line. We made a vast improvement in uniforms! But the development of equipment was far less imaginative. The most important military advance was probably the development of the General Staff idea, with the Chief of Staff as the single center of planning and administrative direction for the land and air forces of the United States.

We learned little about industrial mobilization and war economic institutions from World War I. The M-Day Plan, which was referred to in the second lecture, shows what we did learn, and what we did not learn. We did not have to fight long enough in 1918 to develop a "tight" economy, nor could we imagine what "total war" meant on the basis of those years. As a result, not even the wisest men of authority showed any evidence that they understood the extent of the production and labor controls which are required in modern war. We did get a bitter lesson in inflation, though we did not develop the political or economic statesmanship or national fortitude to apply it after the Spring of 1945. It is rather interesting that the nation, the railroads, and the communication systems learned enough in World War I to avoid government management in World War II. We learned the lesson that an important bottleneck in conversion to war production is the training of foremen and workers, and started the "Training Within Industry" program in September, 1940. The industrialists and labor leaders who took that action not only learned something from World War I, but made an incalculable contribution to the final victory.

Thus, while we profited from our experience in World War I, our failures to learn politically, militarily, industrially and economically, leave us little to be proud of as a nation.

Military Failures of World War II.—In spite of a stupendous final victory, which is the balance sheet of war, we cannot fail to note a number of rather important shortcomings in the management of our military operations. I will refer only to matters in which administration is primarily involved, as neither you nor I can discuss the strictly military side with much profit.

From the standpoint of administration I think we must say that military intelligence left much to be desired. We never knew enough about conditions in enemy and neutral countries. We were badly informed about the character and extent of the damage we had done to German war production, and we had no sufficiently accurate picture of the terrific damage wrought on Japan before the atomic bombs were dropped in Hiroshima and Nagasaki. Perhaps the Joint Chiefs of Staff had the information they needed—though this seems doubtful in connection with the "Bulge," and certain operations in Italy, the Aleutians and the Pacific Islands. But it is clear that our top political and economic strategy and operation were carried forward in semi-darkness for lack of the kind of military intelligence which was required. In spite of the extraordinary work which was done by Army and Naval Military Intelligence, by the Office of Strategic Services, by the State Department, by the Foreign ·Economic Administration, by the Office of Censorship and the OWI, the fact remains that the top command, political and economic, did not have enough accurate information when it needed it. Our intelligence system could not produce it.

It is interesting to speculate on this point. Would Roosevelt have accepted the zone lines in Germany if he had known the probable speed and completeness of German collapse? Would he have yielded so much to draw Russia into the war with Japan, had he known the degree of exhaustion of Japan? Would Stimson and Truman have authorized the use of the atomic bomb in Japan had they known even part of what the Strategic Bombing Survey later disclosed of conditions in Japan? Would Byrnes have encouraged the production hysteria in the winter of 1944-1945 and defeated Nelson's conversion plans, had he known the supply and military situation in Northern France and the conditions in Germany and Japan at the time? In all of these situations, better military intelligence might have changed the course of history.

The second area of failure in military management during World War II is found in the supply picture. This was a complicated situation. Up until December 7, 1941, in spite of tremendous proddings from the White House, the military leaders could not bring themselves to envision even remotely the extent of the prospective supply needs of a total war waged all over the world. This lack of imagination was duplicated by the industrial leaders, and we were told that steel and aluminum capacity, for example, were adequate and that conversion to war production of automobile and other plants was hardly necessary. Had it not been for men like Morgenthau, Henderson, Hopkins, Knudsen, Hillman, Coy, Nathan, Lubin, Nelson and the staff of the NRPB we would never have gotten things shifted to a higher production level until much later. When war came, the picture was completely reversed; the military then knew no bounds in their demands. These demands were beyond the do-able capacity of the economy by March, 1942. At this point the military were not able to translate their requirements into material terms so that production could be planned. When the military programs ran into non-military production requirements and into lend-lease commitments, the military commanders were unable to recognize that a high level of military production could be produced only by a high level civilian economy, and they were unwilling to recognize the comparative priorities involved in the needs of allies under the overall strategy which had been adopted. When it then became necessary to cut back the unreasonable supply and munition programs, the military were not able to produce a balanced program for many months. While Donald Nelson and the civilians who were responsible for the economy were carefully kept in the dark on major military strategy as it affected the supply program, the military did not fill this gap by adjusting their demands with sufficient subtlety to meet strategic needs. The most glaring evidence of this is found in the shortage of landing craft from 1943 to 1945. Though General Marshall mentions this lack several times in his summary report on the war, it was Donald Nelson, and not the military, who learned of the urgent necessities on a trip to England and took steps to speed up the program.[4] Finally the Army, abetted by the Navy, played an important part in destroying the possibility of an orderly transition from war to peace in the American economy. Perhaps this should not be charged up to the military, but rather to the weakness of civilian

[4] Donald M. Nelson, *Arsenal of Democracy*, p. 256.

direction and the economic ignorance of the American people.

Failures in Dealing with Domestic Affairs.—This brings us to consider a third area of failure in the management of World War II, namely the domestic front. As has been indicated, the major failure was our inability to engineer the transition to peace. We did a few intelligent things. We adopted part of an imaginative program for handling demobilization of the GI's. We developed a quick procedure for cancelling contracts, clearing out war goods and machinery and settling claims against the government. We failed to set up an adequate law or administration for disposing of surplus property. We failed to hold the machinery and public confidence which were necessary to prevent post-war inflation, and we were not able to continue the co-operation between labor and management during the period of transition. We failed also to effectuate the housing, clothing and household equipment production called for by returning forces and the war shifts of the American people. Thus our transition from war to peace must be listed as a major series of political, economic, and social blunders on the home front. This will be even more clearly realized as we suffer the consequences of our current post-war inflation, most of which could have been avoided by proper action in 1945 and 1946.

Another failure on the domestic front was the inadequate development of local, voluntary, civilian effort during the war. This may sound like an ungracious statement in view of the millions of man-hours given by patriotic men and women and school children throughout the land, and the indispensable work of the price and draft boards and the USO. Still an analysis will show how far this effort fell short of the possibilities. We spent too much time and education getting ready for improbable bombing raids, and not enough on essential war morale and on individual adjustments to changes in community life, especially on the industrial side and in relation to living arrangements. These voluntary service activities were a valuable feature of war life in England, and in some American communities. But on a national scale we failed to realize the opportunity for action, and as a result failed to release the immense energies which are wrapped up in the community atom, and in the personal relations of individuals.

The worst blunder on the domestic front during the war was, however, our inability to understand and handle the allocation of manpower. As we have already seen, manpower was our final inescapable limiting factor in fighting this war. In spite of this we had no plans when we started which indicated even roughly how many men we would put in the armed forces, on land, sea or air; how many we would need in what kinds of mines, or in what kinds of factories; we did not know how many men we would require in agriculture; we never did have a picture of what manpower was needed to keep power, transportation, and the civilian economy going, or what kind of men we must keep in technical training or in scientific research.

In March, 1942, we were trying to equip an army of 3,600,000 men. By October, the Army was talking about 15,000,000 in the armed services. In November, this number was officially cut to 11,500,-000, of which the Army was assigned 8,248,000. By the middle of 1943, the Army ceiling was cut again to 7,700,000. While these figures themselves throw some light on our muddle-headedness in dealing with the overall allocation of manpower, the method by which the final decision was reached is even more significant. There was never any agency, short of the President, in a position to work out a balanced program of manpower allocation. The WPB was of course deeply concerned with labor for industry, and took strenuous measures to place contracts where labor was available, to close gold mines in the hope that copper, magnesium and other mines would find more miners, to attract women into the factories, to train workers for new jobs, and to press for many other measures designed to meet manpower shortages in industry. But the WPB had no jurisdiction over the size of the Army. The War Manpower Commission, which took over some of the WPB labor activities in April, 1942, was also wrestling with the manpower problems, and had in its directive the authority to:

"a. Formulate plans and programs and establish basic national policies to assure the most effective mobilization and maximum utilization of the Nation's manpower in the prosecution of the war; and issue such policy and operating directives as may be necessary thereto.

"b. Estimate the requirements of manpower for industry; review all other estimates of needs for military, agricultural, and civilian manpower; and direct the several departments and agencies of the Government as to the proper allocation of available manpower."

With all this nominal power, the size of the military forces was not actually determined by the WMC, and it had only illusory directive powers over the Selective Service administration. The Department of Labor drew up composite tables of the total labor force, showing its growth and limits, but it had no authority to act. The Joint Chiefs of Staff which tried to settle the problem was directly concerned solely with the military needs, and at one stage seems to have assumed that the armed forces should claim all able-bodied men between 17 and 45, leaving industry, agriculture, mining, power, transportation, scientific research and future education, and other essential non-military occupations to take pot-luck with what was left over. Though at least five Cabinet members were deeply concerned, not to mention the heads of the major war agencies, the Cabinet did not function as an agency for developing a solution for this problem. Thus it came about that the Bureau of the Budget brought the facts together, stated the issues and the alternatives, and pressed for agreement at the highest levels and for decision by the President.

Even then, we had a firm determination of one factor, the size of the uniformed armed forces, not a general plan of manpower allocation covering all our needs and requirements in a balanced scheme, so designed as to give the most efficient end result.

I am not suggesting that this could have been done perfectly and finally in 1941. We did not know enough about our needs and potentialities and the most effective pattern of allocation until much later. What I am suggesting, however, is that (a) there should have been an authoritative total manpower balance sheet from the very first covering the entire problem, and (b) this should then have been revised from month to month as we gained experience. It follows that there would have been an agency of government, at the President's right hand, with the authority and the prestige required to aid him in making the overall manpower allocation and keeping the manpower resources in balance. For lack of this approach, we went through the war improvising, competing for manpower between essential programs, and precipitating many unnecessary labor bottlenecks, which had to be solved after they had arisen by reversing prior actions. But whatever the cause and whatever the remedy, the fact remains that the most important failure on the domestic front in the management of the war was our inability to understand and to handle the allocation of manpower.

Failures in Dealing with International Affairs.—
Under the leadership of President Roosevelt we held
Russia, China and England in the war through to the
"unconditional surrender" of Germany and Japan.
This was done through national interest, friendly
contacts among the leaders, the supply of US munitions, supporting military actions, and agreement to
accept certain territorial and political arrangements
during the period of occupation and in the peace
treaties.

The President of the United States accepted
these territorial and political arrangements in principle in return for (a) vigorous Russian participation
in the final fighting against Germany and Japan,
so that these countries would each have to fight a
two-front war; (b) a pledge by Russia, and the other
powers, to guarantee the major processes of free
representative government particularly in the fringe
countries of Europe, starting with Poland and
running down through the Balkans; and (c) Russian
agreement to work with us in establishing and
making real use of a new and stronger international organization, after the war, designed to air
international problems and secure their adjustment
without resort to force.

More specific agreements with Russia and England
on the peace settlements should and could have been
reached by President Roosevelt between March 15,
and May, 1945. Many difficulties and strains have

arisen because of this failure, including the un-
planned dismemberment and stripping of Germany,
the division of Korea, the serious bickerings with the
USSR over isolated and often minor details, the
bungling of our broad program for international
loans in the interest of friendship and prosperity,
the initiation of the UN on a keynote of controversy
and bloc action, and the tragic betrayal of the
American demand and the international pledge to
work for the essential processes of representative
government in the fringe countries of Europe.
England shares with us the blame for these failures.

It is not easy to determine where the responsibility
lay for these shortcomings in our international
operations. As will appear further on, our total
achievement in the international field is so spectacular
that it may seem carping to make much of the sins
of omission. I do so because I am convinced that
these failures, like some of the others mentioned
above, have their origin in bad administration.

There were, however, two important factors
which merit special mention at this point. These
were, first, national inexperience which left the
President with little public opinion on which he
could count; and, second, the lack of trained
personnel in the United States not only to handle
international negotiations but even more to develop
the rationale of policy decisions and then to imple-
ment the decisions, once they had been made.

Before we proceed to assess the part which administration played in these failures and shortcomings of our war management—military, domestic and foreign—it is appropriate to give equal attention to our achievements and successes.

MAJOR SUCCESSES

Accordingly we turn to the other side of the balance sheet. There we find: Victory. Though this magic word will balance out all accounts in the long run, politicians will continue to look beneath the surface for irregularities, and students of management may be permitted to seek administrative lessons.

What then were the great successes and achievements? Here again we may anticipate the record of history by attempting to outline these under the following six headings: (1) organization, equipment and direction of the mightiest military force in the history of the world; (2) creation of the required transport; (3) development of an adequate economic foundation for war; (4) the preservation under war conditions of our governmental, economic and social system and of our standards of living; (5) the phenomenal extension of theoretical and applied research not only in atomic energy but in many other fields; and (6) the establishment of comprehensive post-war international governmental machinery. We will now proceed to consider each of these points briefly.

Organization of Fighting Forces.—In four years'

time, from 1940 to 1944, the United States organized
and equipped the most powerful fighting machine
ever put together by a single nation.   In size, we were
not as large as the Russian Army, but our individual
and supporting equipment was so vastly superior to
that of any other forces, that our primacy is without
question.   This was due partly to the quality and
vitality of the manpower on which we were able to
draw, partly to our superior industrial and economic
resources, partly to our organizing and technical
ability, but also to the ability of our military command, the soundness of our top strategy, and the
genius of our field generals in action.

In military operations we far exceeded the
Germans in perfecting speedy mobile land operations,
and solved the problem of amphibious warfare,
which had blocked Germany at the English Channel.
We established complete superiority in the air,
developed new techniques both of offense and of
defense on and over the sea, and showed in the Pacific
that we were proficient under the sea as well.

These colossal achievements were made possible by
hundreds of underlying strokes of genius and good
management, which gave us transport, communications, quick training, better clothing and other
individual equipment, vastly improved medical
services, and superior fighting equipment.

From the management side it should be recorded
that we even achieved a high degree of integration
and singleness of command in most of the fighting

theaters. Once the fighting really got under way,
the top division in military command between the
generals, the admirals and the Army air forces did
not seriously reduce our military effectiveness as
similar divisions did in the case of the Germans and
the Japanese.

Thus we may list the organization, equipment and
management of our air, land and sea forces as an
achievement of the highest significance in the balance
sheet of World War II.

Creation of Transport.—Indispensable to our victory was the speedy development of a gigantic
transport system. This factor has not been given the
attention it deserves. In addition to our naval construction, we built 60,000,000 tons of merchant
shipping, doubling in five years the world's total
investment in ships. We also put 25,000 transport
planes into the air, not counting the bombers we gave
to other countries. Back of every military operation
we set up a transport system of ships, air transports,
pipe lines (directly behind battle lines), and trucks,
trucks, trucks, such as no one could have imagined
before the war.

Nor must it be forgotten that the heart of our
operation was the North American Continent, with
300,000 miles of railroads and one million miles
of hard surfaced highways which were kept at a
high level of operating efficiency through careful
management of freight, rubber and gasoline. To
combat the U-boats, lessen the strain on the railroads

and permit the movement of tankers to other routes, we even built two large capacity pipe lines from the oil fields to the Eastern seaboard.

The creation and maintenance of a world-wide sea, air and land transport system, with its appurtenant communications, and unified management of our home-base transport system are achievements of the highest order.

Development of War Production.—The Germans and the Japanese laughed when President Roosevelt called for "60,000 planes, 45,000 tanks, 20,000 anti-aircraft guns, 8,000,000 tons of shipping" in January, 1942. Even American industrialists and economists thought such a program was beyond the reach of the American economy. But the goal was very nearly achieved, and could have been reached except for changes of design and a greater need for some other items. The total development of our war production from 1939 to 1944 was an industrial feat of the most stupendous order, unmatched by anything in economic history.

This is easy to say, but hard to portray. Still a few figures may help. In 1939, when we started war production in a small way for "defense" and to meet the first foreign orders, the total national product, that is the dollar value of goods and services, was $98.6 billion. In 1944 it was $198.7 billion. This apparent increase of over $100 billion was in part caused by a change in the value of the dollar. If you stick rigidly to 1939 dollars, the increase was 52 per cent in four years! Nothing so impressive ever happened before. If you turn to look only at the extraction of raw materials—iron, aluminum, magnesium, coal, petroleum, food, timber, nitrates, etc. —the increase was 60 per cent. To 1942 we boosted construction—mostly factories and military establishments—by 220 per cent. The chief revolution, however, was in manufacturing. We raised industrial production an average of over 15 per cent a year, so that it stood at 280 per cent of the 1939 figure in 1944. During World War I the increase in industrial production, then considered remarkable, was but 7 per cent a year—another measure of the record achieved in this war.

This record was made possible by an 18.3 per cent increase in the total labor force, in spite of the withdrawals of over 12 million men and women for the armed forces. Manufacturing employment was increased from some 10 million workers to 16.6 million, that is slightly over 65 per cent. The major part of this increase was made up of women, another important phenomenon. On top of this, hours were extended by 20 per cent, and productivity per man hour was raised on an average about 3 per cent to 5 per cent a year, speeding up somewhat a long time trend in the American economy.

While these changes which increased our total production were going on, we were also undergoing another revolution, the shifting over from peace-production to war-production. This can be seen in the following tabulation:

PERCENTAGE OF GROSS NATIONAL PRODUCT
ASSIGNED TO MILITARY AND CIVILIAN PURPOSES
IN 1939 AND 1944

Purpose	1939	1944
Military	2%	40%
Civilian Consumption	70	50
Government and Construction	28	10
	100%	100%

This picture of the distribution of the national effort in 1944 seems to show that the civilian part of the economy was cut down somewhat while the military was greatly increased. There was a reduction of about 30 per cent in the number of industrial workers producing for civilian consumption, but even so, total civilian consumption measured in dollars spent (adjusted to the price level) was not materially reduced. Apparently there was an increase of about 12 per cent over 1939 in quantities, though this was shifted from capital goods to soft goods and food. Thus we did not develop our war production by tightening our belts; we developed our war production by raising our efforts.

This is particularly significant because it represents two extremely important facts: (1) it reflects the American policy in this war of reaching for high production by keeping the civilian economy operating at a high level of essential comfort and efficiency; and (2) it shows that the massive stream of war goods produced, reaching their peak rate of production 24 months after Pearl Harbor, was achieved entirely by increasing the effectiveness of the national economy by leadership, organization, management, the elimination of unemployment, discipline, and national purpose.

Perhaps I am unduly impressed by this experience because I was in the midst of it. But it strikes me now, as I look back with some perspective over the record of what Donald Nelson and the businessmen, the professors and the career administrators did, as one of the major miracles of the war and one of the reasons for our final victory.

Preservation of the American Governmental, Economic and Social System.—Total war has a way of altering governmental, economic and social institutions, especially through the elimination of personal freedom, civil rights and elections, and the substitution of discipline, dictation, and government controlled propaganda, which can be another path from freedom to slavery. Many Americans expected just such a course of events in this country, even going so far as to predict that Congress would be prorogued and that elections would be eliminated.

There were important changes in freedom during the war at five points:

(a) The status of labor in collective bargaining was greatly strengthened. It may be argued that this was not entirely a war development, however, as it grew in part from prior legislation.

(b) The national government did achieve an extremely strong position with reference to world and domestic news, and withheld news and colored facts at times. However, control was enforced almost entirely by public opinion, not by dictatorial restraint. The press was still relatively free, and individuals could say almost anything they wanted to.

(c) Through contracts, loans, priorities, allocations, limitation orders, manpower controls, price controls, wage determinations, rationing, taxation and occasional plant seizures, the government took more or less complete control over the economy and left the indvidual little freedom to "run his own business in his own way." But even so most businessmen could make more money than ever before, and most workers could and did go where they wished and work at what interested them.

(d) The national government enacted and enforced a selective service act, requiring young men who were physically fit to serve in the armed forces. However conscientious objectors were not required to bear arms, and a universal service act proposed by the Army was rejected by Congress.

(e) All Japanese in the country, including United States citizens by birth, were marched from their homes and "relocated" behind barbed wire in the interior, or placed under other restraints, without investigation, indictment, charges or trial.

In spite of these limitations of freedom during the war, limitations which look sweeping and grim when thus catalogued, the United States actually went through this war with a remarkable absence of hysteria, and an extraordinary maintenance of civil rights, freedom and democracy. German and Italian music was never taboo, as German was in 1917; German and Italian language was heard on the streets, almost as in peace time; individuals and the press were free to, and did, criticise the government and its war activities; the elections were held, with normal party activity; Congress and its committees did investigate and criticise war management; and individuals were free in fact to come and go within the country, to work where they wished, or to refrain from working. There were no political "spy hunts," no persecution of minority groups, no "scapegoats," no suspension of jury trials or of other constitutional rights, except in the case of the Japanese on the Coast. Professor R. E. Cushman of Cornell University, a leading authority on our civil rights, remarked:

"It is a significant fact that during World War II, a war in which our national security was imperiled as it had never been before, the only major sacrifices of civil liberty which occurred resulted from military action. We have every right to feel pride and satisfaction in the generally wise and tolerant manner in which the Government dealt with the wartime problems of freedom of speech and press, the treatment of enemy aliens, and, with some qualifications, the handling of conscientious objectors." [5]

So far as the general constitutional structure of government is concerned, the war brought no formal changes except for a time in Hawaii, which was unsuccessfully put under martial law. Executive government in Washington was greatly strengthened as Congress passed sweeping war powers acts and monumental lump-sum appropriations, but no more so than under Lincoln or Wilson, or than the constitution intended from the first in time of war. Toward the end of the war the balance was re-established, with no resistance from the executive. The federal government did take over from the states the management of the Public Employment Service, and exercised considerably expanded influence over state and city governments, directly and through the use of funds and priorities, but these controls were voluntarily yielded, and local authority was promptly restored with the end of the war. Thus it may be said that we maintained the basic American governmental system unimpaired through the war, including democratic controls through elections and public opinion, the federal system with its sovereign states and home rule cities, the function of the courts, and the division of powers between the executive and the legislative branches, both in the national government and in the states. The whole

[5] *The Annals* of the American Academy of Political and Social Science, Vol. 249 (January, 1947), p. 55.

thing was galvanized into unitary action under central leadership, not by constitutional changes or by usurpation, but by a single national purpose and by the force of public opinion. There were no constitutional or permanent changes in our governmental system.

The same may be said of the social system. The family, the community, voluntary organizations, the religious life of the people, and educational systems all went on structurally as in times of peace. What adaptations may be noted were voluntary, temporary and caused by the economic environment and the climate of opinion, not by governmental decree. Major shifts took place in the marriage habits of young men and women, housing standards, college curricula and operating plans, and the buying habits of the people, especially through the elevation of standards of the lower third of the population which enjoyed a new security and rise of income. While the war brought heartaches to a million homes, and many inconveniences and minor deprivations, it is doubtful if the American people as a whole have ever worked so hard and happily, or been so well fed, clothed and housed as from 1941 to 1945.

On the economic side we experienced our greatest controls and changes. In place of allowing the economy to regulate itself through "the market," that is through the decision of individuals dictated by prices and their own idea of a good bargain, we shifted over to controlled prices and government regulation of a large part of the economy through contracts, allocations, priorities and rationing. In the process, many small businesses, especially the repair and service trades and retail and sales outlets were decreased, and the whole competitive system was suspended. But all of this disappeared all too soon for our own good after the war. Such controls as we now have through the tariff, agricultural price supports, minimum wages, and devices designed to keep interest rates low existed before the war. Our free contract system, our wage system, our price system, our free "market," our monetary system, our labor system, even our struggle to prevent "combinations in restraint of trade" have survived the war years, and are again about where they were as economic institutions in 1939. Even the great advance in the bargaining powers of labor is destined to be rolled back somewhat as the result of the November, 1945, elections, and it is too early to say how much of the bulge in higher education will persist after the GI education payments have run out.

During the war the American people learned some very important lessons about their economy. They discovered, for example, as Paul Hoffman, President of the Studebaker Corporation, has said: "We can have full employment in this country and when we do, we can produce all we need and then some." The same idea was expressed by Senator Pepper when he said: "There is no need for unemployment, or poverty, or lack of education or suffering in this country, provided we use our heads, our hearts and our hands with reasonable good sense." This is not only an economic but a political lesson which the American people will not soon forget. It may even prove to be a major economic heritage of this war.

As we look back over the war years, may we not say that the American people waged this war and preserved their governmental system, their social system and their economic system? While adjustments were made during the war, and new drastic controls were established, these were not dictatorial, but had the firm backing of public opinion, and were quickly and easily demobilized with the end of the fighting. And throughout the war personal and civil liberties, free speech and free elections were maintained in a remarkable degree. In comparison with the governmental and economic techniques enforced in other lands during the war, the American record is notable.

Preservation of the National Standard of Living.— A major achievement, already alluded to but deserving special emphasis, is the maintenance of the national standard of living throughout the war years. Here are a few indices:

Total consumer expenditures, measured in adjusted dollars, went up about 12 per cent from 1939 to 1944. As rents were pegged and clothing was limited, a considerable part of this must have gone into more and better food.

The calories of food consumed per capita per day rose from about 3,000 to 3,200.

Meat consumption rose from a prewar average of 126 lbs. per capita in 1939 to 150 lbs. in 1945.

Clothing consumption per capita increased from $44 in 1939 to about $56 in 1944 (at adjusted 1939 prices).

Per capita consumption of shoes went from $9.34 in 1939 to $11.18 in 1942 then dropped to $10.06 in 1944.

Fuel and electricity consumed in homes rose from 33.3 million B.T.U. per capita per year in 1939 to 40.5 in 1944.

Residential crowding was reduced by a drop in the number of persons per dwelling unit—exclusive of farms—from 3.7 in 1939 to 3.3 in 1944.

Wages received by individuals increased from a total of $48 billion in 1939 to $116 billion in 1944 (current prices); while farmers' income went from $4.3 billion to $11.7 billion.

While these are but straws in the wind, they show pretty conclusively that the war did not "blow our house in." We fought the most material-consuming war in history, and at the same time maintained our standard of living at an extraordinary high level. We did forego new autos and household gadgets, and many conveniences, and amusements and comforts, and new clothes and personal service, but we kept up the basic standards. This was done as a matter of high policy, in the belief that this would result in the maximum national effectiveness in war production.

Thus the great expenditures of the United States in this war will be found in the losses and personal suffering of the fighting forces and of their families at home; the inconveniences and aggravation caused by dislocations at home; and the vast exhaustion of the basic irreplaceable natural resources, especially in iron and petroleum.[6]

To fight so gigantic a war without drawing down our total efficiency by impairing our standards of living is an achievement of great importance.

The Advance of Scientific and Applied Research. —One of the great resources a nation must mobilize in a modern war is scientific knowledge, technology, and brains. I am sure that I do not need to recount the story of the atomic bomb to make the point that we scored an achievement in this area as well. This was all the more notable because the scientific achievements were truly international in character. The British and the Canadians joined with us, and former German, Italian and Scandinavian scientists made indispensable contributions.

Because of the histrionic qualities of atomic energy, there is a tendency by the public to overlook the extraordinary progress which was made in other ways. Many electronic advances were made with radar, radio, the proximity fuse, and guided missiles. Medical discoveries revolutionized battle and operational losses and disease, though this war carried us into the tropics. Extraordinary flexibility and dependability were developed for aircraft. A great deal was learned about nutrition and food preservation and transport. Army food and clothing

[6] I do not mention the debt, taxes, or inflation, as these represent not a "cost" but a process of distribution of the burden during and after the war.

were placed on a more scientific basis. Similar advances were achieved in industry, in metallurgy and chemistry, as with artificial rubber and new plastics, though we were not driven to the extremes faced by Germany and Japan in the hunt for synthetics and substitutes. Some day we will look back on these years and appreciate the real importance of the impetus which the war gave to certain types of scientific and applied research, and the way this experience educated the American people to demand government support for scientific research and technological experimentation on a large scale. This whole range of advances, not alone the epochal release of atomic energy, represents another war achievement of importance.

Creation of New International Governmental Machinery.—If war is ever eliminated from the world, it will probably come not as an amorphous fulfillment of the dreams of poets or the prayers of prophets, but through a governmental system created by statesmen. Whether this world government grows by mutual consent or is imposed by force, it is, I believe, inevitable because of man's nature and his inventions. It is truly "one world or none," and there cannot be none, though we may come pretty close to it one of these days, as mankind did once before at the time of Noah and the Great Flood.

Thus even the beginnings of international government can be extraordinarily important. Who knows? Perhaps we are now building in the UN the government which will forever end war! Or make it as rare and limited as internal war in the British Empire. (You see I do not set my standards too high right at first.) Whether we are now seeing in the UN the first gaseous spiral nebula of the new world government, or whether we are witnessing only another more ambitious effort to stop world wars, we must still record the international machinery created during World War II as an achievement of great significance.

During this war we developed international mechanisms for planning and fighting, for allocating resources and assigning finished products. We created international machinery for the administration of relief and the disposal of displaced millions. We set up international machinery for stabilizing exchange and arranging credits and international investments.

Expanding prior organizations, we established international agencies for hastening the development of world standards of health and for creating labor standards, educational and social opportunities, and for dealing with world food, timber and land problems. And finally we created the UN, and set in motion the structure which may in time develop international control over atomic energy, disarmament and private national armies. All of this must be listed as a war-time achievement in which the American people took a position not only of collaboration, but of indispensable leadership.

SUMMARY OF WAR FAILURES AND ACHIEVEMENTS

Earlier in this lecture we paused to note the management failures of the American people and their government in the crisis of 1939 to 1945. As we saw in that review, the American people did not learn much from World War I; we also made some military blunders in managing this war, especially in intelligence and in programming supply needs in relation to strategy; on the domestic front we bungled the transition from war to peace and got badly gummed up in handling our ultimate final resource, manpower; and finally we allowed to slip between our fingers the war-time opportunity to work out international agreements of the deepest significance.

We are now in a position to note also the successes. As we have seen, the American people, in spite of their failures, contributed vastly more than their share toward a final victory. We organized, equipped and managed with originality and skill an army, an air force and a navy of unexampled power; we created a transport system at home and around the world adequate to support this monumental operation; at home we developed war production so fast and so effectively that we were able not only to meet our own needs, but also to give large and indispensable help to our allies. With a population of less than 10 per cent of the world, we seem to have produced almost as much industrially in 1944 and 1945 as all the rest of the world put together. With all this we preserved our governmental, social and economic system; we preserved our national standard of living; we made epochal advances in scientific research and technology; and we took an important part in the development of the new machinery of international government.

It may seem in bad taste to list these achievements as Solomon did when he took a glory-census of his people and incurred the wrath of Jehovah. I do so in great humility, in view of the blunders recorded with equal honesty earlier in this lecture, because we must have the full record before us, before we turn in the next lecture to see what we learned from the standpoint of administration from these trying and important years.

On balance, the total record of the conduct of the war was extraordinarily good. This is a fact. We could have done better and more; but what we did was good enough to win. Perhaps a little self-glorification will not hurt us if we do not inhale!

:IV:

LESSONS OF THE SECOND WORLD WAR
FOR PUBLIC ADMINISTRATION [7]

IN OUR THREE PRIOR MEETINGS WE HAVE considered, first, the history of World War II and the parallel evolution of our governmental agencies designed for the management of that war; second, the nature of the resources which a nation mobilizes in time of war and the way the United States created management machinery to deal with these resources; and third, the successes and failures achieved by the American people through its governmental machinery in the management of World War II. We are now ready to set forth a number of conclusions from this experience which may be stated as "lessons for public administration." In the nature of the case, these "conclusions" are hypotheses, calling for a great deal of further undergirding and analysis, before they are to be considered final or universal, even from the standpoint of the author. However, their statement though tentative may serve the useful purpose of raising discussion and concentrating the evidence.

At the risk of seeming to give unintended and unmerited equal formal rank to the various conclu-

[7] This chapter was delivered in two lectures.

sions, our "lessons" are brought together under 15 numbered headings because this will save words, and enable us to make more progress and speed in dealing with an exceedingly broad and difficult series of ideas.

1. *The American governmental system was found to be fully adequate for the management of the war.*

World War II taught us some important facts about the American constitutional system. Under the inspired and skillful leadership of President Franklin D. Roosevelt our constitution was adequate for the management of the war. Neither the separation of powers, nor federalism, nor freedom of speech, organization and parties, nor elections by the calendar dulled the edge of our sword. Constitutionally our weakest link was clearly Congress, which must take the blame for the inadequate tax policy, the unnecessarily great accumulated debt, and the incipient inflation of which we have not yet seen the end. Our chief war blunder, the failure to prepare for the domestic economic transition to peace, is chargeable both to the Executive and to Congress, and to business and labor, I may add. Woodrow Wilson's difficulties with the Senate, after the last war, seem to have haunted Roosevelt in this war as I have explained, and induced him to make any sacrifice necessary to guarantee unity of action in foreign affairs, even the sacrifice of early planning for an effective program of domestic transition. If this sacrifice was necessary to get Senate backing for

UNO, the Fund and the Bank, and the other agencies of the new international structure, then this too is chargeable to the malfunctioning of Congress in our constitutional system.

During the war, the Presidency as such functioned extraordinarily well from every major point of view. Its greatest contribution was its firm stability and dynamic co-ordinated handling of political leadership, military leadership, international negotiation, and top management of wartime and peacetime agencies of the government, on the foundation of popular consent, freedom and devotion.

The Cabinet as an institution, if indeed it may be called that, continued its dismal course and is not to be listed as an agency of war co-ordination. The White House staff, however, and the auxiliary agencies, those "management arms of the President" which we established in the Government Reorganization in 1939, were on the whole successful. Where would we have been in this war without the Executive Office of the President, without Harry Hopkins in the White House, Justice Byrnes in the White House, Harold Smith and the Budget Bureau in the White House, the NRPB in the White House during the early days, the Executive Secretaries, Assistants and Liaison Officers in the White House, and the whole scheme of the Office for Emergency Management and the National Defense Advisory Committee, in the White House?   It is easy to point to individual blunders, the need for a true "war cabinet" with a secretariat and the "failure" of the system of the anonymous Administrative Assistants, but no one can question the extraordinary total effectiveness of the Presidency under the administrative system which we had through the war years. Perhaps it was luck, perhaps it was Divine lend-lease to the USA, perhaps it was "that Man in the White House"—perhaps the organizational system had something to do with it too. But whatever it was, the American constitutional system *in time of war,* and particularly the Presidency, will long receive the acclaim of historians and statesmen both here and abroad.

2. *A clear statement of purpose universally understood is the outstanding guarantee of effective administration.*

Translated to military terms this is "the mission must be defined." The war taught us that this rule applies not only to the great purposes of national action, but to each specific activity as well. Many have observed that "national unity" created by the fact of war enabled us to carry difficult administrative tasks, like the conversion of the automobile industry to war production, which could never have been shouldered under other circumstances. It is equally true that a crystal clear and realistic statement of mission, as in the case of the Office of Rubber Director, is equally indispensable for effective administration. The lack of such a defined mission for food production has had the results we are now beginning to appreciate. Many a bold war administrator went forth on a white horse only to be mired in the slough of jurisdictional despond because there was no adequate definition of mission in realistic terms, related to the other activities of the government.

On this point military administration taught us a real lesson. With minor exceptions, no activity was initiated by the military without clear definition, a definition cast in terms of purpose, timing and resources; no organizational unit was set up without a statement of its mission. The success or failure of any man or of any venture was measured against this specific statement of objectives and methods. In administration, God helps those administrators who have a clearly defined mission, and thus the beginnings of authority commensurate with their responsibility.

3. *Translation from purpose to program is the crucial step in administration.*

Important as is the statement of a mission and its definition in terms of time, resources and inter-relations, that definition itself accomplishes nothing practically until it is translated into the individual things that are to be done to carry out the mission. While the series of activities which constitute a "program" is perfectly obvious in performing (a) a simple mission, or (b) an oft repeated mission where experience can be the guide, it is a matter of the greatest difficulty in carrying out some substantially novel activity especially if that activity is complicated. In war, most of our missions were totally new to us and were involved, so that their success or failure is a measure of the validity of the techniques used in moving from purpose to performance.

A great deal more study needs to be given to this process of program development. It is a very great art, and demands of administrators not only knowledge and experience in administration, but also the ability to use planning in a high degree and at the same time to act swiftly and energetically on individual matters from day to day so that the decisions fall into a consistent pattern. There is always a strategy of action in which originality and inventiveness are called for because in public administration it is the solution of the new problems which measures the high success of the program, not solely the competent performance of the old activities.

Men differ markedly in their appetite and ability for program development. The planners and professors are generally too inhibited for simple action by their complex intellectual processes; this is also true of professional men generally. The best recruits for this work during the war came from private business and from public life, though business men with all their genius for action were seldom good at dealing with matters of important social and political policy which were at times intermingled with the problems with which they had to deal.

A study of our war experience makes it clear that the central secret of successful program development is the identification of the key controllable item or items in a given situation and then the sure manipulation of those keys. For example, in shifting the economy over to war production what we finally did was to (a) place and finance contracts which gave great incentive to production and conversion, (b) simplify and standardize products, (c) redesign the tax system to encourage war business, (d) prohibit non-war uses of materials and machinery, (e) guarantee or permit the delivery of scarce materials and components only to those who conformed, (f) bring many men from business and labor into government to press for informed and speedy action, and (g) surround management and labor with a co-operative spirit of war enthusiasm. These were the seven keys to war production. The intensely political program to get war contracts into the smaller factories is an excellent illustration of failure in its early days because of the inability of the administrators to discover or lay hold of the key controllable elements. In the earlier days, it seems to have been the conclusion that the solution lay in publicity! The early muddle in war housing was not remedied until an experienced administrator was appointed who decided (a) that the problem was regional in character and (b) that each entire project required a single comprehensive priority.

These are all illustrations of the statement with which I started: translation from purpose to program, from more or less broad objectives to the specific things to be done—this was the crux of administration during the war.

4. *Co-ordination is the indispensable dynamic principle of effective action.*

Co-ordination is not achieved by accident, or by prayer, or by fright, though fear is a great help. Co-ordination must be born in mutual trust and unity of purpose, nurtured in continuous unified planning, and matured in harmonized programming and well-organized routine administration. This, too, is not a new administrative discovery, but its importance to our people was never so clear or vital as in the late war. Without the co-ordination of the Allies there is no doubt that Hitler could have won the war or at least fought it to a draw. Even as it was, he came much closer to winning than most people realize. Without the co-ordination between our fighting arms, on land, air and sea, and the co-ordination that was precariously maintained between our military, lend-lease and civilian production programs; among rubber, gasoline, ships, tanks, landing craft, pipelines, ammunition, textiles, new construction, machine tools, and bottle caps, our total war effectiveness might easily have been reduced by 25 per cent, or 30 per cent, or more. Imperfect though our co-ordination was, it made possible the final surplus of power for all the Allies, and was thus indispensable in the final victory.

Among the administrative tools of co-ordination developed in the United States during the war the most notable were the Joint Chiefs of Staff, the Combined Chiefs of Staff, the Munitions Assignments Board under Harry Hopkins, and the Office of Economic Stabilization and Office of War Mobilization under Mr. Justice Byrnes. Other important co-ordinating activities were performed through the Office of Production Management, the Supply Priorities and Allocations Board, the War Production Board, the National Housing Administration, the Combined Boards, the OWI, the Finletter Committees, the Office of Economic Warfare, the CIAA, the Bureau of the Budget, and the other agencies of the Executive Office of the President. Some extraordinarily important local and regional co-ordination was developed by the Committee on Congested Production Areas and by the Area Production Urgency and Manpower Priorities Committees, adding to the experience we have already gained in localized regional administration through the TVA.

The meetings of the three Commanders-in-Chief —Roosevelt, Stalin and Churchill—though few in number, constituted an international co-ordinating device of the greatest importance in the development of joint military, economic and political strategy. These and other international meetings at

Washington, Moscow, London, Casablanca, Cairo, and Quebec will loom large in the history of this war. To administrators they are significant because they represent a new and extraordinarily important technique of international co-ordination, and the background of much of the co-ordinated programming which followed through other agencies.

At no point in the war is the contrast between the Axis powers and the Allies more pronounced than in the co-ordination they achieved. Germany and Japan were not working for a common victory, they were only fighting common enemies, and were pursuing ends which would have brought them into conflict later. Germany did not help Japan, or Japan Germany, on technical developments like artillery, submarine warfare, radar or air warfare generally.

In contrast, the Allies achieved through co-ordination, imperfect as it was, more strength than they possessed individually. And with all our shortcomings, we achieved within the United States more through co-ordination than we had dreamed was possible.

Not counting unified theatre commands, the best single piece of co-ordination achieved in the American governmental structure during this war, was, in my judgment, the United States Army General Staff. Fortunately the historical origins and the war-time operations of the General Staff have been analyzed in considerable detail by Major

General Otto L. Nelson, Jr. in his *National Security and the General Staff*.[8] There is no need of summarizing the story here, as every student of administration will want to examine General Nelson's report for himself. One point, however, must be mentioned, namely the lesson to be drawn from the *command functions* of the General Staff officers. As General Nelson points out, our war-time experience shows that staff officers in the Army do as a matter of fact participate in command in spite of all the past theory that they are purely "thinking," "planning," and "advisory" agents. This activity extends to formulation of orders, clearance of orders, issuance of orders, and review of execution of orders issued, in accordance with policy decisions of the Chief of Staff as the head of a command. In other words, the staff officers aid the commander in his command functions also. This new functional statement based on actual operations corrects a good deal of past talk about "line and staff," and about the application of line and staff ideas in non-military organizations. In time of war, the military concept of line and staff proved to be quite different from its theory in time of peace. Perhaps administration has more to learn from an Army actively at war than an Army with nothing to do between wars—that is nothing to do except stand around and wait on one side, and make imaginary plans on the other.

[8] Infantry Journal Press, 1946.

When all is said and done, I think the record shows that the General Staff made an indispensable contribution in this war, and that the General Staff idea is applicable not only in military affairs, but also in any large scale management where the functions of the top executive are so broad and his irreducible contacts so far outreach his span of control that one man cannot run the show. In great enterprises must not the top leadership itself be organized? Has any better approach emerged than "the general staff idea"?

Whether this be so or not, I am sure you will agree that this war taught us again that co-ordination is the central dynamic principle of effective action, the hallmark of sterling administration.

5. *Administrative operations may be subjected to control by various techniques other than the limitation of expenditures.*

The major systematic method of exercising administrative control in American government developed up to 1940 was through the control of money. This approach springs from the appropriation process, and has been extended through budget allotments as a tool of central management, and through the audit as a tool of critical supervision.

It remained for the war to demonstrate that there are other types of control, which may be more sensitive and more useful in certain circumstances. During the war, money ceased to be of any significance as a control, because appropriations were unlimited. The shortage factors were manpower, materials, office space, office equipment and time. Therefore administrators soon discovered that controls based on expenditures were of little value, while controls based on manpower, materials, and space; on processes and performance; and on schedules based on time were extremely important. Even Congress sought to establish controls through "personnel ceilings," rather than through appropriations.

In this move to establish new types of administrative control, and to lay a better basis for large-scale supervision and enforcement of co-ordination, government came to apply many of the techniques already explored by industry. In our quest for administrative efficiency in public administration in the future, it would seem that we have a great deal to learn from this war-time experience with new types of administrative control.

6. *Planning is an essential and continuous aspect of management, and is greatly advanced by specialized implementation, though it is difficult to establish stable and effective working relations among planning, programming and operations.*

What we learned about planning as a function of administration during World War II was mostly negative. The plans and designs made in the War and Navy Departments up to 1939 were not too valuable. The administrative plans drawn for

M-Day were quite inappropriate. War was not what the planners thought, and did not come as they had imagined.

All through the war there was extreme difficulty, as I have observed before,[9] in establishing stable and effective working relations between planning, programming, and operations. In spurts, brilliant work was done by the planners; but it was resented by the operators, and was at times too far removed from operations to yield returns. There was a tendency for planners to work in a vacuum or to interfere with programming and operations; and for operators to neglect planning and seek to go their own way avoiding reporting and co-ordination as an unjustified interference with their own responsibilities.

However there were also extraordinarily successful demonstrations of unified planning and execution such as the Normandy invasion, the WPB production buildup, and the development of the atomic bomb. In the first case the men who carried out the operation were, from the first, responsible for the planning and programming. The operators were the planners, and the planners were the operators. In the case of WPB, policy planning evolved from conflicting ideas and purposes arising from the Army, from the operators, from Henderson and his Office of Civilian

[9] *The American Political Science Review,* December, 1944, pp. 1166 ff.

Supply, from organized labor and various pressure groups, from Congress, but especially from the small planning staff—Nathan, Kuznetts, Blaisdell, May and their associates—which was, during the crucial period, an inner element of Donald Nelson's top organization. All this Nelson wove together in making his final policy of production sustained by a high level economy, a policy which, though subject to much criticism at the time, achieved extraordinary results.

In the case of the atomic bomb, research, planning and operations went hand in hand, with the enthusiastic and informed backing of the President, the unhampered activity of the top scientists, the full co-operation and later management assumption on the production side by the Army, and the facilitating co-operation of the WPB. A great deal was gambled on this research, but under continuous scientific, military and political evaluation and review; and a great deal was achieved, far more than the sudden end of the Japanese War, as we shall see in the years that lie ahead. Administrators will find in the official Smyth report on "Atomic Energy" a careful statement of the changing structure of the administrative organization which brought forth the A-Bomb. It is worth more than casual attention.

While one must hesitate to draw any very firm conclusions from this war-time experience with planning, I think it shows that planning is essential; that planning must be done not only before an

operation is launched, but also continuously as it
progresses, in part as a critical self-review; that the
top operators must participate in the process of
planning along with a small specialized staff attached
to the chief administrator; and that the specialized
planners must be given the free run of the organization so that they will not only have all the facts but
will also be compelled to rub their noses in the work
that is going on without getting into administration
themselves. I think we have seen that the planners
need more protection than they were given by the
top administrators whose servants they are. Perhaps
more passion for anonymity on the part of the
planners, and greater passion for planning on the part
of the top administrators and operators is what
public administration needs. On both of these points
the military and the pure scientists did rather better
than the civilian departments.

On one point we must be very clear: there is no
such thing as good operations in any governmental
position, or private occupation, without at least
occasional use of the human brain. If there is such
a post it ought to be turned over to a machine. In
any supervisory position, this brain-work includes
the adaptation of action to meet developing events
and imagining ahead and thinking out a line of
co-ordinated action designed to accomplish a given
purpose. This is what we mean by "planning." It
is an inseparable aspect of doing and living; it can
never be split off from the work of any live admin-

istrator. Those who say they "do not believe in planning" actually plan to improvise and follow a line they do not wish to disclose. "They also plan who only stand and wait." It follows from this that (1) the establishment of specialized planning agencies in no way lessens the planning responsibilities of the operational officers to whom the planning aides are attached though the planners will facilitate the performance of the work, and (2) planning staffs cannot go effectively into problems of future action to a degree which is inappropriate for the officer with whom they are at work. Thus where operations are delegated, the planning of those operations must also be delegated, not only because such plans are inseparable from the operations, but because they are an inappropriate assignment for the delegating authority, and thus for his planning staff.

An aspect of planning in the United States which we should note is the contribution to war administration which was made by the accumulated mass of social, economic and scientific information and thinking in the hands and minds of men skilled in its analysis and use. The cumulative value of the researches of public and private agencies, particularly by university personnel, made a greater contribution to the war than is appreciated. The American penchant for facts and research and the system of private foundations devoted to encouraging and financing research more than justified themselves.

7. *When geographic dispersal of operations calls for decentralization of an organization, high technical standards and policy uniformity can be maintained by integrated dual supervision.*[10]

Most of the war agencies were faced by the necessity of dividing a large part of their work along geographic lines for the simple reason that they had to operate headquarters offices in Washington and at the same time they had to deal with industry, or with the public, or with the merchants, or with the draftees, or with farmers, all over the nation, or with the enemy all over Europe, the Pacific, Africa and Asia. Thus every major agency had a Washington office and a "field organization."

The War Department organized its "field" as "theatre commands" abroad and as "Corps Areas" here at home. The home office had many specialized and technical divisions, such as engineering, medical, ordnance, quartermaster, signal, chaplains, etc. In each theatre command there was a single commanding general. He also had divisions dealing with engineering, medical, ordnance, quartermaster, signal, chaplains, etc. Thus an engineer, or a chaplain, or a doctor in the field had two superiors: he had, first, his commander in the field who told

[10] As here used "decentralization" refers to the assignment of administration to geographic sub-units of a centralized organization, by revokable action of the central organization, under such controls as the central organization may establish.

him where to go, when, and how to team up with
the rest of the Army in the theatre; and second, the
corresponding engineering, chaplain, or medical
service back at Washington, which set his standards
of operation, told him how to do his work,
and on occasion inspected his operations to see
that they conformed to these standards. Thus the
technical services in the field were subjected to
"dual supervision."

The War Production Board divided the United
States into 13 regions, and these into some 100
districts. The organization at Washington differed
markedly from the organization in the field, so that
there was no near similarity at headquarters and in
the field as there was for the Army. The Washington
organization recognized the following major units:
(a) requirements and program units; (b) materials
and industry divisions, such as steel, copper, aluminum, aircraft, shipbuilding, etc.; (c) project or
functional units, such as conservation, scrap drive,
labor, power, and smaller war plants; (d) the
priorities organization, which was in due course tied
to both (a) and (b); and (e) the general administrative services having to do with personnel, budgets,
information, enforcement, etc. In the field, there
were production and expediting engineers, some
lawyers, some information men, and a considerable
force handling priorities papers and giving information to producers. Special units were set up for
some of the special programs under (c) above,

though these programs were generally carried out through the whole field office without creating a special division for the work. One exception to this was the Smaller War Plants setup, which was completely differentiated. From the standpoint of "dual supervision" it will thus be seen that the people in the field had no one technical division at headquarters to give them technical advice, and thus tended to get their orders from various units on various problems. The tendency of central officers to press for action by going direct to the field, ignoring the field organization entirely, or to deal with field specialists direct, ignoring the regional and district chief executives, resulted in considerable confusion, as dual supervision mushroomed out at times into multiple and non-integrated supervision. The situation was, however, greatly improved in time, particularly after priority policies were well defined, and local officers were given authority to pass on priority applications up to specific dollar valuations and to review and decide requests for increased allowances under Controlled Materials Allotments in the case of manufacturers using less than 150 tons of carbon steel per quarter, charging the new allowances against a monthly quota assigned to the regional office.

This assignment of priority power to the field offices illustrates another lesson of decentralization. Though the Washington office was completely swamped by priority applications in the early days, it was thought impossible, for various reasons, to decentralize the right to make decisions on these applications. In the first place no one knew at first even in Washington how strict to be. It was also feared that the local offices might be too generous to their friends and neighbors. This fear proved to be groundless as the local offices were almost universally more strict than the Washington office. A further reason for keeping the decision at Washington was the confidence of top officials in their own judgment. Another reason was the lack of any standard language for sending out policy instructions which would be given the same interpretation throughout the country by local offices even when a policy line was firmly developed. Communication was thus a limiting factor; the WPB at the start had neither a universally understood language for issuing orders, nor a language for reporting activities in the field, which would mirror the effectiveness of programs. Under these conditions, decentralization would have produced not a nation-wide uniform program, or a program which added up to meet national requirements, but a series of local policies, bearing unfairly on different sections and different producers. Later on, when policies were set, precedents established, language defined, personnel educated, experience amassed and reports developed, then it became possible to decentralize important powers of decision with confidence.

Another lesson of decentralized administration

was the value of grass-roots co-operation. Wherever a field office of a Washington agency managed its local activities so as to draw upon the aid and advice of local citizen groups, great values were added to the soundness and efficiency of the total program. This was conspicuously true of the work of the OPA, the WPB, the War Manpower Commission, the Draft Boards and the Agricultural Adjustment Administration. It is extremely important, however, to mobilize the right local leaders and the right interest groups. In the housing field, for example, the final result of co-operation from some real estate groups was a tragic miscarriage of the program. Fortunately this was an exception.

Thus I think we can say that war experience tended to show that activities which must be carried on all over the nation or all over the world must be decentralized. Such decentralization calls for and is limited by the tools and techniques of administrative communication, and requires the development of clearly understood dual supervision in the field together with unified local co-ordination under a "theatre" commander, with a maximum of democratic association with the people of the area and the adaptation of programs to meet local variations effectively.

Dual supervision is aided by the similarity of structure at headquarters and in the field, but rests upon the clearly understood subject matter distinction between (a) the teamwork functions of action

which must be supervised and directed locally, and
(b) the methodology of technical operations which
may be held to standards and supervised by central
technical services and staff agencies.

8. *Broad functional organization is more effective in activities requiring co-ordination than is
organization based on commodities or on specific
operating programs.*

The recurrent agitation during the war designed
to solve operation and production problems by
appointing czars deserves careful scrutiny from the
standpoint of the art and science of administration.
The dominant principle of our war-time organization
may be said to be *functional*. That is, we assigned
fighting and military materiel procurement to the
War and Navy Departments; controlled production
and the use of materials, factories and tools by the
War Production Board; determined prices and
managed rationing through the OPA; supervised
wage and other labor matters through the National
War Labor Board; assigned the overall manpower
question to the War Manpower Commission; gave
the construction, management, allocation and
manning of merchant shipping, to the Maritime
Commission and its off-shoot, the War Shipping
Administration; placed international economic warfare in the Foreign Economic Administration;
assigned the food and agriculture problems to the
War Food Administration and the Department of
Agriculture; vested overseas intelligence chiefly in

the Office of Strategic Services; and assigned domestic information and education chiefly to the OWI. As students of administration know, this kind of organization develops two difficulties: (a) at times individual single-purpose programs and requirements can be seriously neglected, when they fall between the functional stools; and (b) top co-ordination may not be strong enough or well enough informed to maintain thoroughly effective action and timing among the "functions."

We developed both of these weaknesses during the war. Illustrations of the first were the anti-submarine, the rubber, the housing, the food and the fuel programs. Our efforts to get action in these fields after a period of administrative failure and rising public clamor are instructive.

The President threw the submarine problem right back on the Navy where extensive new assignments were made and new techniques developed. On the margin of an extended memorandum to the President from the Admirals on general organizational matters, the President scribbled, "Better leave this to me. Suggest you sink submarines." In any case the submarine crisis was handled within the Navy Department without creating a new independent administration.

In the other special emergency areas referred to, we created new special-purpose administrations. These were the "czars." The best illustration is the Office of Rubber Director.

Even today few people understand what happened in rubber. The initial failure was one of planning and stockpiling. Nobody except William Yandell Elliott was excited about the probable loss of our rubber resources in time to do anything about it. And nobody did enough. Having sustained that irreparable loss, we required an integrated program of conservation, scrap collection, rigid control of use, revision of specifications, price control, release of patents and secret processes, experimentation, determination of production methods, financing and construction of pilot and of mass production plants, experimentation with processing, allocation of critical materials and manpower for expansion of facilities and their operation, and complete international allocation. Among the functional organizations, and in a WPB made up of overlapping industry and commodity divisions, almost every one of these essential steps was assigned to an independent operating unit. Thus the meeting of our critical rubber requirements was falling among a dozen stools.

At this point the public, stirred up by columnists, editorial writers, and others, got excited. The Truman Committee and 16 other Congressional committees aired the facts. Congress passed a law to solve the rubber problem by creating a new completely independent agency reporting directly to the President. This agency was directed to meet all rubber needs and was given power to carry out its

mandate regardless of other programs, with the right
to issue overriding directives. It was also instructed
to use alcohol from agricultural products in its
synthetic program!! Needless to say, the President
vetoed the bill so that the WPB might continue to
"carry on a unified, integrated and efficient program
of war production." However the President recognized the clamor and the need for action and
appointed a notable committee, under the chairman-
ship of Bernard M. Baruch, to review the matter.
This committee quickly produced an authoritative
report, based largely on the program of the WPB's
own rubber co-ordinator. This report put an end to
the conflicting statements of self-appointed experts,
upped the program at some points, and recommended
rationing, extensive reorganization, and the creation
of the Office of Rubber Director. Only strenuous
efforts and fast footwork by the Bureau of the
Budget succeeded in keeping the Rubber Director
nominally within the WPB and thus subject to the
overall priority controls of Donald Nelson. Thus
it was that we set up a czar for rubber, though we
did keep that czar nominally within the priority
system of WPB.

Somewhat the same sequence of events pre-
cipitated the creation of specialized units to deal with
petroleum, coal, food and housing and to protect the
interest of the smaller war plants in war contracts,
though no Congressional legislation was involved
except in the case of the Smaller War Plants Cor-

poration. In every case there was a degree of administrative failure due to falling between the functional stools, a rising tide of public criticism, an effort to solve the problem by setting up a vigorous central management of a special limited program and the announcement of the new administration to the public with great fanfare. But in every case the effort of the proponents to set up a new independent administration reporting to the President and free from WPB priority controls was narrowly defeated, and the integrity of the single, integrated priority system finally maintained.

The other side of this picture is of course the operating experience of the czars. These single-purpose administrators had the great advantage of simplicity of mission. They, their staffs and the public knew exactly what they were trying to do. In general they "got results." They "bulled their way through," overcoming many obstacles. But they also made a great deal of confusion for other programs, as when the Rubber Director upset the timing on the production of 100-octane gasoline and on the escort vessels and on the secret atomic bomb project which were certainly more critical needs than was rubber. The controversy was carried to the President at Casablanca, though the right of WPB to decide the issues was finally upheld.

Thus some people feel that the creation of the czars was a serious organizational blunder. I am not so sure, though I worked very hard to tie the single-purpose administrators into the total picture when I was called to work upon the administrative orders which gave them their power, and am relieved that we had no more czars in the total structure.

In this connection Donald Nelson's method of dealing with the escort vessel program is instructive. Here we had a single-purpose program which was failing with disastrous results. However there was no great public clamor, as the public could not be informed. Therefore Mr. Nelson was free to use a straight administrative cure for the situation. Accordingly he quietly set up his own czar in the person of Lemuel Boulware, and gave him authority to issue any overriding directives he found necessary to get the escort craft program into satisfactory movement. Boulware was an "inside" man, he knew the whole system and the whole co-ordinated end-result sought through WPB. Therefore he solved the problem of the "many stools" for escort ships, and then for landing craft, without upsetting any other programs and with the use of his overriding priority power on only very few occasions. The task was actually no different than the task assigned to the Rubber Director except in size and notoriety. It is to be noted, however, that a special single-purpose energizer and bottleneck-breaker was required in both cases. The task could not be left entirely to the functional structure. It is this which leads me to feel that there are times when a special-purpose approach, rather than a generalized functional approach, is called for. However it is clear that the creation of independent and all-powerful special purpose organizations, that is of genuine czars, must be resisted at any cost. They will do far more damage in a complicated situation than they can possibly counterbalance by their free energy and ruthless drive.

If, however, there are inescapable administrative or political reasons for setting up a czar, the top command must at the same time greatly strengthen the co-ordinating structure and be prepared to use it. Any other course will lead to chaos.

9. *The danger of overloading the chief administrative officers is greatly increased in time of national emergency.*

All top officials whom I had an opportunity to observe had more to do than they could possibly encompass with satisfaction to themselves. They had more divisions and agencies reporting to them than they could possibly direct or supervise. They saw more people and talked about more problems than any man could possibly give attention to. They were involved in more interdepartmental committees and conferences than they could prepare for, attend, or participate in effectively. They were all pressed by events, public relations and congressional contacts and hearings. In most cases, the executives were driven by emergencies rather than by their own energies and programs. An interesting indication of this is the fact that most executives had three-quarters of their time or more taken up with appointments others made with them, rather than with appointments which they made on their own initiative. From this standpoint, the best organized offices in Washington during the war were the War and Navy Departments, the Maritime Commission, Harry Hopkins' office, and the Bureau of the Budget.

Wherever the span of control was stretched beyond any reasonable practical limit, the result was inability to cover the whole field of responsibility, attention primarily to elements of pressing immediate concern, the tragic development of unnecessary internal jurisdictional and personal conflicts, and the neglect of future problems until the future was upon us. It is my personal belief that the violation in the White House of the doctrine of limitation of the span of control is responsible more than any one factor, except the death of President Roosevelt, for our national unpreparedness for the transition from war to peace.

It must be admitted, however, that the work load of war, even when the structure of the organization helps to limit the span of attention, as in the office of the Chief of Staff of the Army, imposes a superhuman load on every key man. This is inescapable. For this very reason, organization in time of emergency needs to make allowance for the overload which emergency itself creates.

10. *Competent personnel is, of course, indispensable, and the creative administrative genius is*

priceless. Nothing is so important except perhaps clear and sound policy direction.

We learned some important lessons, both old and new, about personnel during the war. Millions of men and women came forward to offer their loyal service to the government. This was reassuring. But even so, it was hard to find, as Patterson French said at Princeton, "people with perspective and insight into the nature of the governmental process; leaders without biases; and people who know how to run an organization." I would add to this list: men with the temperament of decision, *and at the same time* happy to accept democratic processes and controls.

Though we made great improvement in civil service administration by delegation to operating departments and decentralization geographically, and the establishment of new machinery for reaching scientific and administrative personnel, still we found that the search for manpower followed in the main the old chain of personal acquaintance and too often drew only on the available pools of unemployed persons. Serious doubts were raised as to the adequacy of our professional education, because of its over-compartmentalization without a compensating integration along the periphery of the specialties of knowledge and experience. But even so, men and women working in hastily assembled teams, dealing with completely new activities, accomplished wonders, their energies released by new opportunities and high morale.

Thus the war gave us not only a keen recognition of the importance of personnel, and a searching test of our civil service techniques, but also good experience with new techniques, a test of our educational system as such, and a new basis for appraising the importance of the teamwork and morale aspects of human endeavor.

11. *The War gave us a new recognition of the importance of time in the administrative process.*

Though administrators have always been driven to meet deadlines, imposed by budget dates, fiscal years, legislative sessions, tax calendars and periodic reports, administration has seldom faced time pressures of such crucial force as in this war. The landing in Normandy itself might have been impossible three months later as the rockets came into full play and as German war industry went underground. What if we had taken our time at a leisurely pace, while Germany developed the atomic bomb? Those were deadlines indeed!

The element of time was found to be not just something on the clock or calendar, but it was the precise equivalent of steel and copper and aluminum; it was ships, aircraft, 100 octane gas and rubber. In the allocation of these critical materials, upon which the date of the invasion itself depended, a million tons in one month was found to be only 500,000 tons in two months; it was time that made the difference. But it was precisely time which we could not afford, and which we had to allocate and apportion along with aluminum and steel and manpower.

Time came into the administrative picture in another way. It put a great premium on the elimination of red tape, as in personnel practices and procurement procedure, and in encouraging direct action across the lines by administrative subordinates, as reflected in General Somervell's famous order to do away with "layering."

Many of the devices of normal administration are designed to protect individuals against arbitrary official action and to protect the government against fraud or overcharge. When time is no great object, these ends may be sought by advance hearings, competitive bids on contracts, advance advertising, pre-audits, delay in the taking effect of administrative rules, arbitration in case of dispute, review and ratification of plans before action, extensive interdepartmental clearances, and other similar devices. When time was short, we found many ways of short-cutting these procedures without seriously sacrificing the individual and governmental protections involved. For example, when we did away with competitive bids on contracts, we made provision for subsequent renegotiation and for recapture of excess profits by taxation. When we established arbitrary WPB controls, we provided for an elaborate system of appeals within the WPB; when we cut rations drastically, we appointed local boards of review to deal with hardship cases. In these ways we made possible prompt and ruthless action, but we provided for subsequent remedies, appeals and audits.

The success of these procedures is an important lesson for those who are concerned with the time factor in administration. This approach would have saved a great deal of time, for example, in the original PWA program in the early days of the depression.

Another effect of the lack of time was the impossibility of waiting for "things to work themselves out," that is for the normal processes of evolution. We have always recognized that administration is compounded of three indispensable elements: purpose, organization and manpower. Some have said that of these three, the only important one is manpower, because good men can fix the organization, or secure a new definition of purpose. War experience did not bear this out. Good men seldom survive bad organization. In this situation, time again played an important part. Perhaps the high value of time is something which we have overlooked in administration.

12. *International administration at the consultative level presents no new problems or principles with which we have not already had experience in the United States in our domestic affairs.*

International administration does, however, accentuate certain problems which arise in all administration, such as:

(a) the problem of agreed terminology, which is seriously affected by differences in language, concepts and ideals;

(b) the passion for "sovereignty" and for "face

saving," which we know already in milder form in states rights and home rule, and maneuvering for political "credit";

(c) the need for orderly committee management, including procedural rules, agenda, preparation of material, conduct of meetings, formalizing the results, and especially maintenance of the impartial committee secretariat, an art greatly in need of development in our own administration;

(d) the problem of unified guiding principles and delegation of authority to negotiating officials;

(e) the double difficulty of international and geographical apportionment of personnel appointments and their reconciliation with service needs; and

(f) the problem of public relations and public reaction in connection with administration, a matter which is doubly baffling in international affairs, because of differences in cultural and governmental systems.

While these six aspects of administration assume greater importance in international administration than they do in straight domestic administration, I think you will agree that they do not constitute problems which are unknown or unimportant in our own past experience. And I can assure you, after working with the representatives of a score of nations over the last five years in Washington, London, Paris, Brussels, Moscow, Berlin, Tokyo and Manila, that the administrative arts which bring success are no different in the international field than in the domestic field, though they do call for more patience, tact, and imagination.

One more word needs to be said about the importance of the co-ordination of all aspects of a nation's dealings with another nation. At various times during the war, nothing was so disconcerting as the lack of a single co-ordinated policy for the various parts of our government which were dealing with foreign governments. Many a time the War Department was going one direction, as when it took ships out of the Latin American trade, when other agencies were headed in other directions, as when the WPB needed tin from Bolivia, the Co-ordinator of Inter-American Affairs was trying to maintain friendly relations in Latin-America, and the Board for Economic Warfare was making deals to strangle Nazi interests. Similarly the American representatives on the Combined Food Board, the Interim Commission for Food and Agriculture, and UNRRA were often at cross purposes, for lack of an integrated national policy. We have finally been forced to recognize the supreme necessity of unified theatre commands in military affairs. Our war experience teaches us that there is equal need for unifed political and economic policies in dealing with any unified geographic area. This aspect of international relations will call for far more attention than it has received thus far in the government of the United States. The development of functional specialization through the functional departments, like the Treasury, Commerce and Labor and of co-ordination of all foreign contacts through the State Department without duplication of specialists, presents an administrative problem of great difficulty and corresponding importance. This problem of organization and co-ordination has been greatly sharpened by our new role in international affairs.

13. *The support of public opinion is essential for good administration under American conditions.*

Without the generally informed support of public opinion in this country public administration is extremely difficult if not impossible. We learned this again and again during the war. The number of administrative difficulties and impossibilities which were dissolved overnight on December 7, 1941, is spectacular. Without overwhelming public support, the draft could never have been enforced. The controls of the WPB over materials and production, and of the Manpower Commission over workers not only would have been unworkable without mass acceptance, but would probably have produced just the opposite results from those which were sought, but for that support. An excellent case in point was price control. All through the war, we achieved a high degree of success in spite of legislative delays and management blunders. When a minor but powerful segment of national opinion shifted against control at the end of the fighting, the whole system was thrown into disrepute, many of the price controls started to produce artificial shortages, and the

administration fell apart. If nothing else makes us
a self-governing democracy, the impossibility of
enforcing programs which lack general public
backing may be said to guarantee the force of
public opinion in this land. If our recent war
experience is a sound guide, it is doubtful whether
even substantial majorities can enforce nation-wide
programs in the face of minority disaffection.
Perhaps this makes our democracy more a negative
protection than a positive and dynamic force,
contradicting Macaulay's famous dictum that our
constitution is "all sail and no anchor."

The price of popular support for public administration involves respect for mankind and a continuous
process of taking the public into one's confidence.
This is a hard lesson, particularly for businessmen
who serve the government only during a war
emergency. It requires a special aptitude and skill
developed only in public life. Except for the political
gold fish, working for the public "in a gold fish
bowl" cannot be other than an aggravating and
disconcerting experience, like painting a landscape,
writing a poem, sinking a crucial putt, or proposing
to a young lady with a talkative crowd looking over
your shoulder and making humorous suggestions.
The irresponsible writings of special columnists,
which seem so often to be inspired more by the desire
to stir up personal conflict and news than to tell the
truth or inform the public, is particularly hard to
endure. There are essential processes of government

which cannot be performed in public, especially the negotiation of workable compromises between embattled interest groups and the preliminary elaboration of policies and programs. There are also governmental actions in which timing is an important factor, or in which justice requires that no one shall have advance knowledge of facts or proposed actions. Still it is not safe in the long run to let governmental officials decide for themselves what part of their conduct is and what is not suitable for public exposure. Without doubt more is gained for democracy and sanity by exposure than is lost through irresponsible journalism. Thus we must adhere rigidly and dogmatically to the doctrine of the freedom of the press even though international, political and public libel are beyond effective control, and the competitive nature of journalism makes it difficult to develop responsibility. Once again we must put our faith in education and the gradual rise of mass standards. If this faith is not justified, our whole adventure in self government will probably fail.

14. *Official representatives of organized interest groups are apparently more useful as advisers and as salesmen for government programs than as routine members of the administration.*

During the war we experimented again, as in the days of the NRA, with interest group representation within the structure of government. The War Labor Board had businessmen as representatives of industry, labor leaders as representatives of workers, and professors, politicians and public officials as representatives of "the public." Similarly labor leaders of high standing served in the OPM, the WPB, on the advisory board of the OWMR and especially in the War Manpower Commission. Farmers were represented on various advisory groups of the War Food Administration and the Department of Agriculture by the officers of agricultural organizations, and bankers helped the Treasury on bond sales. In two important areas, our war administrations were actually operated by the officers of the already organized private industry: these were the Petroleum Administration for War and the Office of Defense Transportation, though each of these agencies operated officially under the hand of an experienced public servant—Secretary Ickes for the PAW, and Joseph B. Eastman for the railroads. In all other cases, the officers and paid secretaries of organized industry were specifically excluded as a matter of policy from $1 a year employment or from appointment on industry advisory committees as in WPB and OPA.

What did we learn from this experimentation? It is hard to say, though several observations may be made. Where the industry was drawn in to run itself, as with the railroads and petroleum, relations between the government and the industry were smooth and efficient. It was extremely important, however, to have public servants at the very top able to see and deal vigorously with the internal rivalries of the industry, and at the same time to draw out and use broad and patriotic industry leadership.

From the standpoint of achieving maximum effectiveness in war, members of an industry were at times too concerned with the post-war production and competitive situation, to make the best judges of what was to be done during the war. Good illustrations are the struggles over steel and aluminum expansion and over the Big and Little-Inch pipe lines. However, all-in-all, the industrialists were far more open-minded and public spirited than were the representatives of agriculture who teamed up with their politician allies more than once clearly against the public interest and price control.

The value of participation by labor leaders could not be fully tested because of the internal conflicts within labor, especially between the CIO and AFL. Another difficulty with labor participation arose from the critical shortage of experienced and trusted labor personnel. Few labor leaders could afford to drop their labor union activities and work continuously within the government, apparently because of political insecurity within their own organizations. Thus, with few exceptions, labor participation was limited to the occasional meetings of advisory bodies. In these posts labor made important contributions to the total program, not solely to its organized labor phases, and labor participation served also to mobilize labor acceptance for the various programs involved. Many a plan of the WPB, the WMC, the WLB and the OWMR might have been wrecked by labor except for the fine work which was done from the inside by the representatives of labor in perfecting the program initially, and then in selling the program to the workers of the nation. With a few exceptions, labor leadership and labor economists worked hard to avoid inflation, at least until the end of the fighting. In this regard the leadership seems to have been far more literate economically than the membership.

These experiences seem to indicate that there are both dangers and positive gains from bringing into the government official representatives of organized interest groups. The dangers are found in the inability of such representatives to appreciate the public interest, and the tendency to bring into the government the internal power squabbles existing within the interest group. These dangers can be mitigated by placing at the official head of an organization a public servant of political sagacity, ability and energy, and by using the representatives of interest groups as advisers on policy matters, not as integral parts of the administration. The gains from interest group participation were of two types: first, advice in developing practical and acceptable programs; and second, assistance in selling programs to the membership of the interest group. Both of these services, again, may best be performed when the interest-group representatives are advisers, rather than operating members of the administration. This does not mean that men with a railroad background, or a labor background, or a banking background, or a petroleum industry background should not be employed within the administrative hierarchy of the national government; but it does seem to indicate that such men when employed for administrative work in government should be recruited directly by the government, not designated by the organized interest group, and should then sever their relations with the interest group and become public servants fully and completely. This is, of course, not interest group representation, but rather the employment of public servants who have specialized knowledge of a given field which happens to be organized on the basis of its interests.[11]

[11] Consumer representation was initiated at the very beginning of the "defense" period, and continued through the war in the effort to guarantee that the consumers would be protected as the economy moved over onto a war footing. A member of the National Defense Advisory Commission was designated "Advisor on Consumer Protection," in May, 1940. This office was included in the Office of Price Administration and Civilian Supply in April, 1941, and was transferred to the OPM and then to the WPB when that agency was created in January, 1942. However the OPA established the post of Consumer Relations Adviser, and at one stage appointed an "ordinary consumer and housewife" to advise the Price Administrator. The Department of Commerce, in the National Bureau of Standards, also maintained specific representatives of "consumers" in the development of its grade labeling and other standards.

"Consumer protection" within the WPB had a .checkered career. In the early days the "Office of Civilian Supply" was chiefly protecting the consumer by urging a more all-out war

This brings me to the final administrative lesson which I wish to draw from World War II. It is this:

15. *Truly effective action in administration arises from singleness of purpose and clarity of policy, ardently believed in both by the leaders and by the public in all parts of the country and in all strata of society.*

I shall not elaborate this point because it is implicit in most of the other conclusions I have advanced. Still it is a matter of such importance and places such a responsibility upon political leaders and upon top administrators that I cannot fail to give it this added emphasis. Leadership alone does not produce this

---

effort through conversion of auto plants to aircraft production, etc., thus protecting the consumer against the Germans and the Japanese. Later on, after becoming the Office of Civilian Requirements, the agency did protect the maintenance, repair and operation needs of American industry against over-allot-ments to the military and to lend-lease, and began to develop some semblance of a production program for clothing, house-keeping supplies and other strictly civilian requirements. At the end the program did aid the consumer both through the defense of civilian needs and through the efforts to secure more production of the low price commodities.

But taken as a whole, throughout the war, the major defense of the civilian against unnecessary hardships came more as a result of the central policy decision of the Chairman of the WPB and the President than through any specific defense of his rights and interests by "consumer" representatives. Apparently the real defense of the consumer comes not from special interest representation so much as from broad economic policies based on the public interest as distinct from the special interest of some producer, processor, distributor or user group.

unity of national purpose, though it contributes to it. Such purpose and policy spring from the culture of a people under the impact of events. Those who make up a nation are conditioned by the past, by the environment, by education and by the insights of great leaders of thought and action. When there is no unity of purpose and policy, administration alone cannot make up the deficiency; when purpose and policy are antagonistic, administration will fail; but when a nation drives forward with unity of purpose, then administration can accomplish the impossible. This is precisely what America did in World War II.

SUMMARY

What then were the administrative lessons which we should take to heart from World War II? Most of them were not new lessons, though they do present new aspects. You will see this as I run over the list again in summary:

The American constitutional system and the management system established under it showed great resiliency and strength under the test of total war.

The Presidency, with the 1939 structural improvements, acquitted itself brilliantly. The weakest link in our government was Congress, though the executive branch must share part of the blame for our greatest blunder, the bad transition from war to peace.

A clear statement of purpose in terms of time,

resources and interrelations is the outstanding guarantee of effective administration.

The translation from purpose to program is the crucial step in administration, a process which involves the identification of the key controllable elements in a given situation and then the sure manipulation of those few keys.

Co-ordination, that is the dynamic interrelation of purpose, organization and manpower, is essential, and makes possible an achievement far beyond the sum total of the elements combined. Of all the structural approaches to co-ordination, the general staff idea proved the most fruitful.

Techniques of control other than the financial can be developed and are highly useful in large scale organizations.

Planning cannot be separated from operations, or operations from planning. The best results were secured with planning agencies established in accordance with the general staff idea.

Decentralization is essential. It is conditioned by communications and requires not only regional co-ordination, but a clear application of the doctrine of dual supervision, and the introduction of grass-roots co-operation.

We learned the uses and the dangers of czars in war administration, and found that broad functional organization is more effective in activities requiring careful co-ordination. If czars are found necessary for special administrative or political reasons, it is wise to strengthen the co-ordinating machinery by means of which the czars are held to their assignments and restrained from doing more damage than they do good.

The danger of overloading top administrators is greatly increased in time of emergency. Many of our war-time difficulties can be traced to the undue extension of the span of control.

The war taught us again the pervasive importance of good personnel. We moved ahead years in our civil service techniques, particularly in the delegation of functions, and we saw even more clearly than before the meaning of teamwork and the value of high morale. Certain weaknesses of our educational and social systems came to light also, particularly over-compartmentalization without the balancing force of a generalized insight into the nature of democratic processes and the structure of the national interest. We seem to be directing our best brains into specialized techniques and narrow group interests, and leading too few into the integrating techniques and generalized public concerns.

The war gave us a new recognition of the value of time in administration.

International administration, we discovered, rests on the same administrative arts and procedures as does other administration. However in international activities, a number of special administrative problems are accented such as terminology, the desire for independent credit, delegation, committee management, the apportionment of personnel, public relations and the development of unified national policies. Experience to date throws little light on the problem presented in organizing international executive power.

Under American conditions, the support of public opinion is essential for good administration. Interest group representation can aid in perfecting programs and securing public support, but is to be used in administration only with caution.

Truly effective action in administration arises from singleness of national purpose and clarity of policy, ardently believed in by leaders, by administrators, and by the public in all parts of the country and in all strata of society.

These, I believe, are the more important permanent lessons which students of administration may draw from American management experience during World War II.

EPILOGUE

One cannot conclude this discussion, standing here beneath the portrait of Thomas Jefferson, without saying a word about democracy and World War II.

The Fascist adventurers in Germany, Italy and Japan were convinced that the doctrines of democracy would make it impossible for the democratic nations, and especially for the United States, to act in time or with sufficient concert to prevent the complete success of their policy of overwhelming one nation at a time.

The Hitler and the Tojo views of the United States were not flattering. We were selfish and incapable of clear thinking or sacrifice; too "ethical" and "moral" for a world of power-politics; and incapable of quick or effective national action even in our own defense because under democracy we were divided by our polyglot society and under capitalism deadlocked by our conflicting private economic interests. We were moreover weakened by Christianity and Pacifism, an easy prey to propaganda, softened by prosperity, and afraid to fight.

This diagnosis of America, of democracy and of private capitalism as a social and political system was a major central assumption of the German and of the Japanese high commands. They not only told their people, "with many a sniggering jest," that we would not and could not fight, but *they believed it themselves and made their economic and military plans accordingly.*

Under the circumstances it is instructive to examine the comparative effectiveness of the totalitarian and the democratic nations in the war.

CLAIMED SUPERIORITIES OF TOTALITARIAN DICTATORSHIP

The administrative advantages claimed for dictatorship in time of war are based on two approaches. The first insists that dictatorship is free of democracy's delays, divided counsels, inertia, and conflicts between entrenched interest groups, and is not limited by the low mentality and disabilities of the "average man." The second claim of superiority is more positive. It asserts that dictatorships, resting on a single "leader" and a small highly integrated elite, alone have the ability to make adequate and far-seeing plans; to integrate and co-ordinate the economy; to act with vigor, intelligence and dispatch; to interrelate military, political and economic strategy; to master timing and surprise, protected by complete control over secrecy of action; and to develop fanatic national unity and enthusiasm.

WARTIME DISCLOSURES

I hope all Americans will read the summaries of the reports of the Strategic Bombing Survey on Germany and Japan, and the final chapter of the Budget Bureau's *The United States at War.*[12] In these reports they will find that these totalitarian "superiorities" are bogus claims. Neither Germany nor Japan freed themselves from the weaknesses listed, nor achieved the positive virtues claimed. In both categories, Great Britain, Canada and the United States showed fewer weaknesses and greater strengths than did the three Axis governments.

[12] *The Effects of Strategic Bombing on the German War Economy,* Government Printing Office, 1945; *The Effects of Strategic Bombing on the Japanese War Economy,* Government Printing Office, 1946; *The United States at War,* Government Printing Office, 1946.

This is not the time or the place to document this assertion in detail.   But a few observations may be in order.

First of all we may look at the soundness and completeness of the fundamental plans.   Both Germany and Japan, though they selected the dates to start the fighting and were successful beyond their dreams at first, completely misjudged the eventual developments and the military requirements.   The action of the totalitarian leaders was irresponsible and disastrous in the nth degree.

Next is the question of top manpower.   In Germany the ablest administrators were displaced, relegated to secondary roles, or withdrew to safe positions from which some plotted the assassination of Hitler, and the advice of the ablest military leaders was consistently ignored.   In Japan every responsible administrator or military man who knew the Occident was pushed out of power because his informed cautions were *non grata*.   In the democracies, the outpouring of skilled and able manpower from business, from the universities, from the professions, into government was extraordinary and extremely effective.   Though this could have been handled more expertly, the record is still impressive.

As to the speed of military and industrial mobilization, and the magnitude of the effort realized in relation to the available resources, the record of the democracies is notably better than the record of the dictatorships.   The comparative failure of Germany and Japan at this point arose from inadequate initial planning, inadequate integration of the military production programs, the tardy development of controls over the industrial economy, the selfish behavior of entrenched cartels and favored politicians and the failure to recognize blunders and make adjustments.

Germany pre-eminently, and Japan to a lesser extent, were supposed to possess and use technologists and scientists in the development of their war machines and methods. With a long and deliberate head start they did outdo us at the beginning. And Germany did evolve improvements in rockets, submarines, jet planes, and possibly tanks, of some importance. But in the short time allowed us we made rather more progress in amphibious warfare, radar, atomic fission, bombers, motorized transport, military medicine, and the technology of war production. The democracies clearly outdid the dictatorships in the use of technology and science.

The greatest superiority of the free peoples, however, arose from two things: the superiority of their broad plans and their elasticity, their quickness to change in the face of need. I think it requires no argument to show that these two superiorities spring directly from the democratic process. Broad plans are more valid when they have been subject to the kind of review and criticism which democracy alone affords. Broad plans which are hatched in secret by a small group of partially informed men and then enforced through dictatorial authority are likely to contain fatal weaknesses, undetected until too late. Wide discussion and criticism bring to a plan an indispensable preliminary testing, and avoid many a disaster. The delay caused by debate in wartime America was considerably less than the delay caused by poorly considered and unrefined and inadequate programs in Germany; and no American blunders of broad war planning were as disastrous as half a dozen major German errors. Not a few of the errors which Germany made, such as underestimating early commitments, overbuilding factories and machine tools, dividing the priority power, underestimating the need for the expansion of basic materials and power, were avoided in this country only by the democratic process and outspoken public criticism of official proposals.

The superior flexibility of the democracies in the face of developments is easy to understand when the record is analyzed. In dictatorships decisions are made by the leadership group. They are enforced with ruthlessness. Neither criticisms nor constructive suggestions are wanted or heeded. "Failures" are hidden and denied behind a wall of censorship and discipline. Even the leaders tend to believe their own propaganda. All of the stream of authority and information is from the top down. Thus the first evidence of need for change, which occurs inevitably at the lowest echelons of the Army, of the economy, or of society, has no way of communicating itself to the high command. The channel of command in a dictatorship is a one way street. In a democracy, not only is the structure of administration designed to flow both ways, with extensive delegation of authority and universal participation in planning and decisions at every level of the organizational structure, but in addition the public and the press have no hesitation in observing and criticising the first evidence of failure once a program has been put into operation. Thus democracy establishes two channels of communication between the lowest echelons of administration and the top command, one within the government, and one through public opinion. Such a system is far less likely to suffer from a hardening of the arteries, than is the entrenched bureaucracy of a dictatorship.

We have always supposed that a major superiority of the democratic system in time of war would be found in the unity of the nation and the eagerness of all free men to fight for their country. We assumed also that dictatorships might find considerable difficulty at home. The Nazis, on the other hand, expected that the democracies would be torn with dissension and afflicted with disgruntled citizen groups.

The war experience threw some light on these problems. Before the issue was drawn, the Nazis did succeed in organizing Fifth Columns in certain countries. Apparently they were right as to what can be done with ambitious men and disgruntled elements of a population before war issues have been drawn or the nature of the plot made clear to average minds. The next lesson is Canada, where a geographically centered, highly political population group did prevent conscription for overseas service, but did not lessen appreciably the ultimate national contribution to the war. This experience requires much further analysis. Then there was the United States, which was galvanized into a national unity by the Japanese attack at Pearl Harbor in a most spectacular fashion. Nothing was lacking in the national unity which was thus established. Even the Japanese, the Germans and the Italians in this country, with extremely few exceptions, rallied to the American cause with devotion and enthusiasm.

It is a sobering thought that the peoples in the totalitarian countries were no less loyal and enthusiastic. The gregarious social impulses of men around the world are apparently much the same, giving rise to the same reactions of group loyalty when men are subjected to the same true or imagined group threats.

In World War I, the German homefront was seriously undermined by propaganda even when the German armies were everywhere still on foreign soil. Nothing of that sort was evident in this war. Evidently the techniques of managing mass morale were carried to such a point in Germany and Japan —with the aid of foreign bombing, of course—as to make domestic morale all but impervious to foreign suggestion, even in the face of evident military collapse.

I conclude from these observations on mass behavior of peoples under dictatorship, that dictatorship of itself does not seem to lessen their loyalty or readiness to work or die for their masters, provided those masters understand the arts of mass psychology. While the record shows that the dictatorships were less efficient in this war, I see no evidence that the lack of national morale or the distrust of the average man is one of the causes. This is a sad discovery, but one worth noting for the record.

IN CONCLUSION

Why have I brought this series of lectures on war administration to a close by discussing the comparative successes and failures of democracy and dictatorship as shown in the administrative management of this war? Because I want you to grasp the central fact which this war experience drives home: that good administration and democracy are not incompatible. They are inseparable allies; neither can exist or survive long without the other. I hope you will note and reflect on the administrative lessons I have endeavored to draw from our management of the war; but most of all, when men come to you with doubts over the administrative efficiency of democracy and over a large measure of freedom and private enterprise, I hope you will remember the experience of these war years.

Don't sell Thomas Jefferson short!

APPENDIX

KEY TO ABBREVIATIONS

AAA   Agricultural Adjustment Administration

Ag   Agriculture Department

AExC   Administrator of Export Control

ANMB   Army-Navy Munitions Board

APC   Office of Alien Property Custodian

APUC   Area Production Urgency Committees, WPB

ARC   American Red Cross

ASF   Army Service Forces

BB   Budget Bureau

BEO   Board of Economic Operations

BEW   Board of Economic Warfare

BuA   Bureau of Aviation, Navy Department

BuS   Bureau of Ships, Navy Department

BWC   Board of War Communications

CAP   Civil Air Patrol

CAS   Division of Central Administrative Services

CCC   Commodity Credit Corporation

CCPA   Committee for Congested Production Areas

CCS   Combined Chiefs of Staff, United States and Great Britain

CD   Control Division, ASF

CFB   Combined Food Board, United States, United Kingdom and Canada

CG   Coast Guard, Treasury Department

CHC   Central Housing Committee

CHW   Co-ordinator of Health, Welfare and Related Activities

CI   Co-ordinator of Information

CIAA   Office of Co-ordinator of Inter-American Affairs

CMA   Coal Mines Administration

CMP   Controlled Materials Plan

CND   Council of National Defense

Com   Commerce Department

CPF   Committee on Physical Fitness

CPRB   Combined Production and Resources Board, United States, Great Britain and Canada

CRMB   Combined Raw Materials Board, United States and Great Britain

CSAB   Combined Shipping Adjustment Board, United States and Great Britain

C & O   Commander in Chief and Chief of Naval Operations, United States Fleet

DAR   Division of Defense Aid Reports

DCB   Defense Communications Board

DDHC   Division of Defense Housing Co-ordination

DHC   Defense Housing Co-ordinator of the Advisory Commission

DPC   Defense Plant Corporation

DSC   Defense Supplies Corporation

EDB   Economic Defense Board

FCC	Federal Communications Commission	OCWS	Office of Community War Services
FEA	Foreign Economic Administration	ODHW	Office of Defense Health and Welfare Services
FEPC	Committee on Fair Employment Practices	ODT	Office of Defense Transportation
FSA	Federal Security Agency	OEM	Office for Emergency Management
FWA	Federal Works Agency		
HMC	Health and Medical Committee	OES	Office of Economic Stabilization
ICC	Interstate Commerce Commission	OFF	Office of Facts and Figures
		OFRRO	Office of Foreign Relief and Rehabilitation
IADB	Inter-American Defense Board	OGR	Office of Government Reports
Inf	Division of Information		
Int	Interior Department	OIAA	Office of Inter-American Affairs
JCS	Joint Chiefs of Staff		
JD	Justice Department	OLLA	Office of Lend Lease Administration
Lab	Labor Department		
MAB	Munitions Assignments Board, United States and Great Britain	OOP	Office of Organizational Planning, WPB
		OPA	Office of Price Administration
MInsp	Bureau of Marine Inspection, Commerce Department	OPACS	Office of Price Administration and Civilian Supply
MRC	Metals Reserve Company	OPCW	Office of Petroleum Co-ordinator for National Defense
ND	Navy Department		
NDAC	National Defense Advisory Commission	OPM	Office of Production Management
NDMB	National Defense Mediation Board	OPRD	Office of Production Research and Development
NHA	National Housing Agency	OPS	Organization Planning Staff, PAW
NRC	National Research Council		
NRPB	National Resources Planning Board	ORD	Office of the Rubber Director
NWLB	National War Labor Board	OSRD	Office of Scientific Research and Development
OC	Office of Censorship		
OCD	Office of Civilian Defense	OSS	Office of Strategic Services
OCS	Office of Contract Settlement	OWI	Office of War Information
		OWM	Office of War Mobilization

OWMR Office of War Mobilization and Reconversion

PAW Petroleum Administration for War

PBCND Priorities Board of Council of National Defense

PRC Petroleum Reserves Corporation

PWRC Presidents War Relief Control Board

P & M Procurement and Material, Navy Department

RDC Rubber Development Corporation

RFC Reconstruction Finance Corporation

RRA Retraining and Reemployment Administration

RRC Rubber Reserve Company

SFAW Solid Fuels Administration for War

SFCW Solid Fuels Co-ordinator for War

SPAB Supply Priorities and Allocations Board

SSS Selective Service System

StD State Department

SWPA Surplus War Property Administration

SWPC Smaller War Plants Corporation

to ND Transferred to Navy Department

Treas Treasury Department

TWI Training Within Industry Service

UNRRA United Nations Relief and Rehabilitation Administration

USCC United States Commercial Company

USES United States Employment Service

USHA United States Housing Authority

USMC United States Maritime Commission

USO United Service Organizations (Private)

USPHS United States Public Health Service

USTC United States Tariff Commission

WCPAB War Contracts Price Adjustment Board

WD War Department

WFA War Food Administration

WMC War Manpower Commission

WPB War Production Board

WPU War Projects Unit, Bureau of the Budget (end of 1942)

WRA War Relocation Authority

WRB War Refugee Board

WSA War Shipping Administration

XOP Executive Office of the President, the White House

INDEX